WHAT ARE THEY
THINKING?!

WHAT ARE THEY
THINKING?!

The Straight Facts About
the Risk-Taking, Social-Networking,
Still-Developing Teen Brain

AARON M. WHITE, PhD

SCOTT SWARTZWELDER, PhD

W. W. NORTON & COMPANY

New York • London

For information about permission to reproduce selections from this book,
write to Permissions, W. W. Norton & Company, Inc.,
500 Fifth Avenue, New York, NY 10110

For information about special discounts for bulk purchases, please contact
W. W. Norton Special Sales at specialsales@wwnorton.com or 800-233-4830

Manufacturing by Quad Graphics

Book design by Chris Welch

Production manager: Louise Mattarelliano

Library of Congress Cataloging-in-Publication Data

White, Aaron M.

What are they thinking?! : the straight facts about the risk-taking, social-networking,
still-developing teen brain / Aaron M. White, PhD, Scott Swartzwelder, PhD. —
First edition.

pages cm

Includes bibliographical references and index.

ISBN 978-0-393-06580-0 (pbk.)

1. Adolescent psychology. 2. Adolescence. I. Swartzwelder, Scott. II. Title.

BF724.W42 2013

155.5'13—dc23

2012048066

W. W. Norton & Company, Inc.

500 Fifth Avenue, New York, N.Y. 10110

www.wwnorton.com

W. W. Norton & Company Ltd.

Castle House, 75/76 Wells Street, London W1T 3QT

1 2 3 4 5 6 7 8 9 0

To our families

Contents

Chapter 6: **THE DIGITAL WORLD** 149

Chapter 7: **SEX AND SEXUALITY** 173

Chapter 8: **DRUGS** 192

Chapter 9: VIOLENCE   221

AFTERWORD   245

WHAT ARE THEY
THINKING?!

Preface

If life were a rafting trip, adolescence would be the rapids. Wild, untamed, lots of fun, and, if you're not prepared ... dangerous. Adolescence can be a tumultuous stage of life for parents, teenagers, and innocent bystanders. If you're an adult, take a moment to remember what a huge pain in the butt you were to your parents during your own adolescence. For those of us who are parents of adolescents now, it's our turn to contend with the whirlwind changes in behavior and emotions that characterize much of the second decade of life.

Teens are neurologically driven to push away from adults and become independent. This helps them get ready to leave the nest, and use their newly learned skill sets to forge an adult life. However, this thirst for independence can be confusing for everyone involved, resulting in heavy sighs, sarcastic eye-rolls, tantrums, brooding silences, teeth-gnashings, threats, groundings, and desperate ultimatums. The good news is that recent science can help us understand adolescence better, particularly the changes in brain function that drive typical teenagers to rebel, to take risks, and to reject their parents. We know. Between us, we have thirty years of neurobiological research on brain differences between adolescents and adults. Our lab was the first to show that alcohol affects memory-related brain circuits differently in adolescents than in adults. We've published dozens of scientific papers, spoken at numerous conferences, and addressed parents all over the country on the subject of the teen brain. But we are also parents. Scott has three children in their late teens through early twenties, whose brains are still developing. Aaron has two preteens that are taking their first steps into adolescence.

You might be surprised to learn that the term "adolescence," used to describe a distinct stage of development, was coined only about one hundred years ago—in 1904, to be exact, by psychologist G. Stanley Hall. He referred to it as a period of "storm and stress" that was characterized by intense mood swings and conflict with parents and other authority figures. So the concept of a specific transitional stage of development between childhood and adulthood is relatively new.

What's even newer is the idea that the teenage brain is still developing. When we were taught neurobiology, the accepted science told us that the brain was pretty much finished developing by about the age of ten, and that little changed thereafter until things started to decline during old age. Boy, were they wrong! During the past fifteen years, neuroscience has shown that the teen brain is wired for the often tumultuous transition into adulthood, and that it is built to learn. It's like a living lump of clay, molded by interactions between the individual and the outside world. Each adolescent adapts to the demands of his or her particular environment and tries to learn how to thrive in it.

As scientists, we've been following the emerging research

on adolescent brain development for seventeen years. This knowledge has helped us immensely as parents to understand the differences between ourselves and our pre-adolescent and adolescent children. But until recently, that research was not developed enough to enable us to responsibly interpret issues that adolescents face. There has now been enough research to allow us to share this incredibly valuable and sometimes startling information. The research we're about to present not only demystifies teen mood swings and unusual behavior for concerned (and confused) parents, but will also help parents develop science-based strategies for shepherding their teens through these stormy years.

Adolescence is a relatively brief period, but it affects how we think, feel, and behave for the rest of our lives. Many of the psychological and physiological brain changes of adolescence serve as double-edged swords, providing great opportunity and great risk. The people your kids meet and choose to hang out (or not hang out) with, the classes they take, their exercise and eating habits, the TV shows and movies they watch, the games they play, and the substances they ingest all mold the brain into its adult form. Once adolescence ends, the ability of the brain to change diminishes significantly; we lean on the experiences of adolescence to guide our behavior and choices for decades to come. Understanding how the adolescent brain works and changes, and the larger purpose of adolescence as a stage of development, makes it easier for adults to help their teens' brains to develop in healthy ways, and to prevent teens from damaging their brains through unhealthy behavior.

We're now going to explore the adolescent brain: how it works, how it changes, how it learns, and how to keep it healthy. We'll cover a wide range of topics that are important during adolescence, and we'll do it through the lens of the latest, state-of-the-art brain science. We hope that by sharing what science is saying about the adolescent brain, we can give teens and the adults in their lives some guideposts to help everyone survive adolescence in one piece, and to help teens reach their full potential.

The task of raising a teen, or sometimes simply having a conversation with one, is further complicated by the fact that the world keeps changing, so each generation of adolescents brings its own styles, habits, social issues, and looks to the dinner table. While you may have refused to cut your hair and insisted on listening to Led Zeppelin at eardrum-busting volume, today's teens may text during dinner and play video games that are so violent your heart starts racing with only a glance in their direction. Teens also think differently from adults (literally!), which can lead to generation gaps marked by differences in attitude, beliefs, behaviors, and language. These gaps help convince adolescents that the adults around them are out of touch and hopelessly square. And usually they're, like, totally right! However, brain science has shown that although language, clothing, and other cultural factors change over time, many of the highlights and pitfalls awaiting adolescents remain similar generation after generation. Understanding the teen brain from a scientific point of view can help adults figure out how to guide teens through familiar hurdles despite divisive generation gaps.

Yes, there are all kinds of things that will keep us tossing and turning throughout our kids' teenage years. When they haven't called, texted, or tweeted, the alarm bells will go off and many of us are sure to lose our tempers, throw up our hands and scream, "What are you *thinking*?!" But understanding what's going on in your teen's ever-changing brain can go a long way toward understanding exactly what he is indeed thinking, and making sure that adolescent rafting trip is a pleasure ride with rapids everyone can handle.

Chapter 1

TEENS AND THEIR BRAINS

When does a child become an adult, a girl become a woman, a boy become a man? In Victorian England, the legal age of marriage for men was fourteen, for women, twelve. In Jewish culture, a boy becomes a man at the age of thirteen. In America, right now, eleven-year-olds are tried for murder as adults. In every culture, all over the world, we expect teenagers to be capable of acting all grown up. But, in actuality, our teenagers' brains are in the midst of all kinds of change, and adulthood is not yet in their grasp.

During the teen years, the brain transitions from dependence on adults to relative autonomy, as we move from being children raised by adults to adults able to raise children. Today, the teen years fall within the period of human development called adolescence—a transitional stage between the dependence of childhood and the independence of the adult years. The time span of adolescence can be defined according to hormonal, behavioral, social, or brain changes, so it is notoriously difficult to pin down. We believe that it is less important to specify the precise years of adolescence than to understand it as a period of biological and social transition that is driven largely by brain development. Generally, though, this transition occurs between the ages of ten and twenty-four.

While often fraught with anxiety, peril, and many moments of dazed confusion, adolescence is also a crucial time for self-discovery and personal growth. During adolescence, it is a teenager's job to learn how to take care of herself and make her own decisions, as she separates from and becomes less dependent on parents and other adults. Teens explore the world, socialize with peers, text relentlessly, share their silliest selves and sometimes their deepest secrets with friends in social cliques. They don't want their parents hanging around with them anymore. They can be secretive, break curfews, and become champion eye-rollers. The eventual aim of this exploration and sometimes clueless rebellion is to be able to function with relative independence.

The adolescent urge to flee the nest is actually a biological imperative, not a behavioral or personality-driven choice. Our very DNA is screaming: "Get me out of here!" One of the most fundamental and powerful of these biological urges is reproduction. Making babies is right up there with avoiding death when it comes to making sure human beings stick around year after year. But if two closely related individuals reproduce, their children will likely carry genetic combinations that could compromise their survival and their own capacity to reproduce. In order to keep people from having sex with close relatives, therefore, nature has made a developmental period when young people have not only the strong urge, but also the physical capacity to leave the environment in which they were raised and to hook up and hang out with a whole new group of people.

Risk-taking is another powerful biological imperative. Being a teenager is all about taking risks—they drive faster, take more drugs, push social limits, and challenge authority, while most adults settle into a lifestyle that seems awfully boring by comparison. Risk-taking comes from the desire to explore the world and to find out how things work. The fact that the urge to take chances is strong during adolescence, when the brain is elastic and primed for learning, explains why this time of exploration and experimentation is an opportunity for neurological and psychological growth—as well as a dangerous period for teens who don't know when to say when. In fact, risk-taking might be the single best example of the role of brain development in the transition from dependence to independence, from being a child to being an adult. Tough as it may be to accept for many parents, risk-taking gets your teenager out of the living room and into the world. It helps teens interact with and earn the respect of peers. Risk-taking also helps build confidence and facilitates the drive toward independence.

The separation process and the inevitable conflict that accompanies it are normal and, if handled properly, healthy. While this has been true for millennia, today the rocky road to independence can be stressful and confusing, given the staggering array of both opportunities and pitfalls awaiting teens.

A Work in Progress

During the teen years, the brain is highly plastic, moldable, and sponge-like so that it can soak up as much information as possible. As adolescents explore the world and try on different identities, their brains absorb and retain new experiences, ideas, and skills with great ease. During adolescence, the habits we pick up, the abilities we master, and the memories we hold on to have a big impact on the quality of our adult lives— on who we become and whether we have happy, productive futures. By taking a tour of the teen brain and of the many recent discoveries made about this awe-inspiring organ, we can begin to understand why the teenage years are so important and influential. We can also see why teenagers are so difficult to parent.

It was long presumed that the brain stopped developing after the ripe old age of ten. By that time, many basic social and cognitive functions, like empathy and language skills, are established, and skills such as learning a new language become much harder. The brain also reaches its peak physical size around this age. Because everyone assumed the brain didn't grow after childhood, it was believed that the risk-taking, rule-breaking, and general tumult of teenagehood stemmed from the puberty-based bombardment of hormones—the physical metamorphosis that prepares the body for creating and protecting children. We now know that while hormones certainly do contribute to the roller coaster ride of adolescence, they are just a piece of the puzzle. Thanks in part to research by Dr. Jay Giedd and colleagues at the National Institute of Mental Health, and to the development of powerful brain imaging techniques, it has become clear that the organization and functioning of the brain changes radically during the adolescent years.

Magnetic Resonance Imaging, or MRI, has allowed scientists to learn an incredible amount about the teen brain. Researchers and clinicians now use such technologies to assess the structures and functions of the brain in far greater detail than older imaging techniques like CAT scans could provide. Functional Magnetic Resonance Imaging, or fMRI, is a related technique that allows us to study how and where the brain processes information while people perform various tasks, think various thoughts, and feel various feelings. The combination of these techniques, MRI and fMRI, lets us measure how brain structure changes during adolescence and how the teen brain handles different tasks at different ages. Such studies reveal that the antiquated idea of adolescence as a quiescent time in terms of brain development is far from accurate. In reality, it is a time of massive rewiring.

The changes being discovered by researchers are unique to adolescence and are not an extension of the way the brain develops in childhood. These changes are responsible for the problems teens have with predicting consequences and making forward-thinking decisions; why they seem stuck on emotional overload; why they find drugs so alluring; and why the teen years are so volatile. On the plus side, these changes also help teens develop social skills, the ability to solve complex problems, the mental flexibility needed to learn to drive a car, hold a job, and plan for the future, as well as successfully pay a mortgage on time every month. Ultimately, it's the changes in brain wiring, and not simply hormones, that make adolescence such a distinct period of development.

WHAT'S GOING ON INSIDE YOUR HEAD?

The human body is a vast colony of trillions of individual cells, all desperately trying to work together to keep us alive and to help us accomplish tasks. The brain is a control area, with structures that organize the activity of the body's cells, make sure those cells' needs are being met, and guide the body toward objectives such as breathing, eating, drinking, e-mailing, and making babies. The basic layout of the brain is established by genes, but the wiring is also dependent upon experience. The malleability of the developing brain allows young people to adjust to the demands and requirements of their environments, increasing their odds of success during adulthood.

The brain is remarkably complex and still poorly understood. Hundreds of billions of neurons, one of the two key types of cells in the brain, communicate with one another using chemical messengers that influence moment-to-moment changes in brain processing, behavior, and the way we think and feel. Glial cells, the other main type of brain cell, do many things, including speeding up the signals that go from one neuron to the next, promoting the transfer of oxygen and nutrients to neurons, and getting rid of dead cells so that the brain's environment remains clear. They also nurture and sustain neurons by holding them in place, feeding them partially metabolized glucose (sugar) for fuel, and fighting immune battles. And they form a key part of the blood–brain barrier, an intricate system of blood vessels and cells in the brain that filters the blood so that only essential and nontoxic chemicals can get close to brain cells.

The brain can be divided into areas with very different functions. Some are involved in seeing, others with learning, being afraid, or experiencing pleasure. Parts of the brain located closer to the base of the skull are devoted to keeping us alive; they control reflexive and nonconscious functions like breathing, heart rate, yawning, gagging, and sleep and wake cycles. The closer one gets to the top of the head, particularly the top of the head closer to the forehead, the more complicated, abstract, and humanlike the brain functions become. They include thinking, chatting, making to-do lists, daydreaming, solving quadratic equations, pondering one's existence, and figuring out whether to eat another chili dog.

Some animals come into the world with brains already programmed to do the things needed for survival. This is somewhat true for humans, too, but the human brain has an amazing ability to modify itself in major ways depending on what happens after birth. This is best reflected in how quickly newborns go from being slobbering blobs to reaching out and grabbing noses, crawling, walking, talking, and borrowing money from Mom and Dad. The human brain has evolved to take a gamble on the notion that the experiences the individual has after birth will be more beneficial to survival than a preprogrammed plan for how to function in the world. Given how many humans there are on the planet, the gamble seems to be paying off.

The Frontal Lobes: Captains of the Ship

Some of the most intriguing neurological changes of adolescence take place in the frontal lobes. Located just behind the forehead and above the eyes, they play a critical role in memory, intentional movement, impulse control, decision-making, planning for the future, language, the ability to stop watching YouTube videos of cute cats, and other higher-order cognitive functions. The frontal lobes are the captains of our ship. They coordinate, promote, and suppress the actions of other brain areas as we make plans and decisions. More than any other brain structures, they are responsible for our success or failure as adult humans. The frontal lobes are engaged when we're thinking about ourselves and the world, trying to understand what others are thinking and feeling, and controlling deep-seated urges that may conflict with religious values, societal rules, and our own best interests. Indeed, it is the abundance of frontal lobe tissue, and the resulting ability to self-reflect and think abstractly, that separates humans from even the most sophisticated nonhuman species.

If you've ever watched a teenager in action, you know it can be difficult for them to weigh consequences, make forward-thinking decisions, and control impulses. If you ask a fourteen-year-old why she got high in the bathroom at school knowing full well she'd get caught and she answers, "I don't know," that might actually be the truth. The fact is that her frontal lobes are undergoing wild changes that strongly affect her ability to do the right thing in the face of temptation.

At roughly the age of eleven for girls and twelve for boys, the volume of frontal lobe gray matter peaks and then declines throughout adolescence and into young adulthood. "Gray matter" gets its name from its dark appearance, which results from tightly packed collections of nerve cell bodies—the part of the neuron that contains the genetic and metabolic machinery that keeps cells running smoothly. But although the cell bodies do much of the basic work, it is the cell's axon—a long thread-like structure stretching out from the cell body—that allows neurons to communicate with other cells and create biological networks that process information, make decisions, and control behavior. Axons act rather like electrical cables; they are wrapped with insulation so that they can carry messages farther and faster. That insulation—called myelin—is very light in color, so bundles of axons that carry information from one group of cells to another are called "white matter."

It might seem counterintuitive that frontal lobe gray matter volume increases during childhood and then *decreases* during adolescence. But we now know that during childhood, neurons in the frontal lobes overgrow and form far more points of communication (called synapses) with other neurons than will be needed for adult life. It's like going to a party and frantically meeting everyone. Over the course of the evening you will winnow down the list of people you'd like to get to know based on common interests, backgrounds, and fashion choices. But introducing yourself to everyone is an important part of the process. The original overgrowth of neurons creates a lot of new contacts but far fewer will remain once the pruning process is complete.

As childhood draws to a close and adolescence begins, the brain switches from overproduction mode to selection mode. Just as our brain cells are becoming more selective and fine-tuned to the others with which they communicate, we go from rushing around meeting everyone at the party to zeroing in on those we want to stay in touch with. During adolescence the brain stops overproducing synapses in the frontal lobes and puts many existing synapses on the chopping block. Hundreds of billions of points of communication will be sacrificed during the teen years. As we begin weeding out synapses, frontal lobe circuits exercised through experience get stronger while underused connections are eliminated, leading to a reduction in gray matter. Only those synapses that form meaningful, useful points of contact will be kept. If a teenager reads lots of books, the book-reading connections will prosper and solidify. If a teenager smokes a lot of cigarettes, the cigarette-smoking connections will become dominant. Shaped and molded by a teen's experiences, the frontal lobes acquire a configuration that will carry the individual, whether she reads books or smokes cigarettes, through the adult years.

As frontal lobe gray matter increases during childhood, the metabolism (or energy use) of the frontal lobes increases as well. Fueling the frontal lobes of a child takes tons of energy. During early adolescence, the amount of energy required by the frontal lobes decreases, due to the decreasing number of synapses, and reaches adult levels by the age of sixteen to eighteen. However, declines in gray matter volume and energy usage in teenage brains does not mean the frontal lobes are not working as hard. In fact, there appears to be an increase in reliance on the frontal lobes to organize and control behavior as we move from the troubled teens into young adulthood. As the volume of gray matter and metabolism decrease, brain activity during frontal-lobe-dependent tasks such as problem-solving or planning becomes more focused and efficient and the accuracy of performance improves.

Because the frontal lobes regulate so much of the brain, the changes taking place there in adolescence affect overall brain function, making more complex behaviors and subtle thinking possible. This process allows us to adapt to the environment and to enter young adulthood with cultural rules and life lessons embedded in our brain circuitry. As the frontal lobes mature, adolescents naturally get better at doing the kinds of things that the frontal lobes control, such as making good decisions about the future and controlling impulses. Until that process is complete, however, adolescents will continue to make decisions that baffle, shock, and occasionally mortify adults. For instance, research indicates that teenagers tend to choose immediate, small rewards over large rewards that they have to wait for, while adults tend to go for the bigger rewards down the road. For most adults, it just seems logical to delay gratification and choose the bigger payoff later. If a pair of shoes we really want will go on sale in a few weeks, it's better to wait for the sale than buy now. However, with the impediment of immature frontal lobes, teens are lured toward quick rewards. Saving money for college is probably going to seem lame to a teen when a pop-up ad for a brand-new X-Box stares at him every time he opens his computer.

Beyond the Frontal Lobes

The frontal lobes are part of the neocortex, which means "new covering." The neocortex is the multilayered brain tissue that blankets the top of the brain and generates its sea-spongey, pruny look. It is what most people picture when they visualize the brain. But the brain is actually divided into several distinct lobes, including the famous frontal lobes, the less well-known parietal lobes (on the sides of the brain), the distant but crucial occipital lobes (at the very back of the brain), and the curvaceous temporal lobes which bend around the lower part of each hemisphere like the thumb of a boxing glove.

As with the frontal lobes, the amount of gray matter in the parietal lobes peaks around age eleven and decreases throughout adolescence. Located on the sides and toward the back of the brain, the parietal lobes are primarily involved in processing physical sensations, such as touch and spatial relationships, including where the body is relative to other objects nearby. They also play an important role in interpreting and creating music, solving math problems, and other higher-order abstract cognitive functions.

The temporal lobes, right behind the temples, process complex sounds like words, music, and cell phone ringtones. The temporal lobes also contain the hippocampus, critical for storing new information. The volume of gray matter in the temporal lobes plateaus at age sixteen to seventeen. Although neurons are always dying off naturally, recent studies show that new neurons in the hippocampus are born throughout our lifetimes. Memorizing the statistics of everyone on the

New York Yankees, or learning a new word every day, seems to work in the same way as exercising a muscle with weights. But during adolescence no such exercise is needed; the hippocampus is firing on all cylinders. The circuits in the teenage hippocampus change in response to stimuli so readily that adolescents really are built to learn.

Memories stored with the help of the hippocampus are called autobiographical because they refer to what we've done and learned—such as whether we had a bran muffin or a Pop-Tart for breakfast, or that we haven't done our homework and need to do a cram session on Wikipedia. The skills we learn, like riding a bicycle or typing on a keyboard, are different and involve other brain regions. Without a hippocampus, a person cannot make new autobiographical memories; if you introduced yourself to someone with a dinged-up hippocampus, left the room, and came back, they would likely swear they'd never met you before.

While much of the heavy lifting associated with learning and memory is carried out by the hippocampus and the temporal lobes, they, like many other brain regions, are influenced by the frontal lobes. We not only have to be able to learn and to remember (abilities largely made possible by temporal lobe structures like the hippocampus), but we also have to make decisions—conscious or not—about what to learn and what to do with those memories. During the adolescent transition to adulthood, these varied functions come increasingly under the control of the frontal lobes, so that learning, planning, and emotional self-regulation can be integrated in ways that allow the adolescent to make plans and set goals.

Dogs sniff, bunnies listen, humans look. We are visual

animals. Smell, touch, and taste are important, but we ori-
ent ourselves by sight and use this sense nearly all the time.
More than 80 percent of the neocortex is involved in vision
in one way or another. The occipital lobes, at the back of the
brain, are the vision masters. The retina, a layer of specialized
cells on the interior surface at the back of the eyeball, picks
up information from light bouncing off objects, converts that
into neural signals, and relays them mainly to the occipital
lobes. The cells and circuits in the occipital lobes decipher this
information and put it together into complex patterns, colors,
depth, and distance perceptions. The occipital lobes then send
this partially processed information to the parietal lobes, temporal lobes, and frontal lobes for a final touch-up, thus creating
a conscious experience of perception.

Visual perception and the learning associated with it are
subtle but vital brain functions. The volume of gray matter in
the occipital lobes increases throughout adolescence and into
the early twenties (in contrast to what happens in many other
brain regions), allowing for visual information processing to
become better and better. Although it is not clear exactly how
this late brain maturation affects visual functioning, it means,
at least, that adolescents are processing visual information
somewhat differently from adults. Whether this increases
the likelihood of adolescents crashing cars is still to be determined. But it's important to understand that the visual system
is changing during adolescence and may be more susceptible
to external influences—such as long hours in front of a computer screen—as it develops.

White Matter Matters

Most research on adolescent brain development has focused on changes in gray matter. However, there are also changes taking place in the other major category of brain matter: white matter.

While the volume of gray matter peaks early in adolescence, the volume of white matter appears to keep increasing throughout adolescence and into young adulthood. This increase in white matter is due, in part, to a process called myelination. As the brain matures through adolescence, the axons of nerve cells become wrapped in a fatty insulation called myelin, which is produced by cells known as glial cells. The process of myelination results in faster processing in brain circuitry and quicker communication between brain circuits. But there is a price to pay: the changes that allow for this speedier processing also make it harder for the brain circuits to reorganize themselves based on experience. So, adult brain circuits might function faster and more efficiently, but the ability to change and adapt is not as great as in the adolescent brain. The formation of new neural circuits based on experience, followed by myelination which locks those circuits in, allows the developing brain to learn a new language lickety-split. Once myelination takes place, it is harder to learn a new language and most of us will speak it with an accent. It's also what causes that memory of your first kiss to remain so vivid and vibrant, while you can't for the life of you remember your boss's wife's name, even though you've been introduced numerous times. The strategy employed by the brain appears to be this: learn fast and hard as we move toward adulthood; myelinate the resulting brain circuits to allow for expert execution of the skills learned during adolescence; then protect these circuits from being overwritten or lost as life proceeds. This is great when teens are learning all kinds of new, useful skills. But, as we'll see, it's not so ideal if adolescent experiences involve a great deal of pain and trauma or if all they learn is how to play drinking games, watch TV, and text at rapid-fire speed.

Given the importance of myelination, it makes sense that the more white matter volume the teenage brain can manufacture, the stronger cognitive and emotional development will be. One example of this is "working memory", the ability to keep information like a new crush's phone number active in your memory even as you're making up a story to tell your parents about where you were and why you're late for dinner again. As the adolescent brain matures and the circuits connecting the frontal lobes and other areas involved in memory become solidified, the ability to pull off this mental magic just gets better and better.

The thickness of the corpus callosum, a bundle of myelinated axons connecting the left and right hemispheres of the brain, also increases during adolescence, eventually (and some would say predictably) reaching a larger size in females than in males. The corpus callosum is important in organizing behavior. When the corpus callosum is cut in procedures designed to prevent seizure activity in one side of the brain from spreading to the other, signals are blocked, and the two sides of the brain can actually end up competing for control of the person's actions. For instance, you might try to button a shirt with one hand while your other hand tries to unbutton it. The left hand might literally not know what the right hand is doing. Increased thickness in a healthy corpus callosum reflects increased myelination of axons, which allows the two sides of the brain to chat faster and more efficiently.

As white matter in the corpus callosum increases during adolescence, certain cognitive functions, such as acquiring vocabulary, reading, and the ability to work with complex visual and spatial information, improve. This is particularly true for the splenium, a portion of the corpus callosum that connects visual processing areas on the two sides of the brain and reaches full maturity during the college years—later than other regions of the corpus callosum. It is significant that a brain function as fundamental as the communication between the two cerebral hemispheres is still developing during what was very recently considered "adulthood."

Show Some Emotion

Thinking and reasoning are all well and good, but emotions make us aware of being alive, and therefore make us human. This integration of thinking and feeling is one of the highest-order brain functions, and is crucial to our ability to thrive in the emotionally and intellectually complex world of adulthood. But we're not born with this ability. A four-year-old is often overcome by emotions so powerful she can do nothing but collapse in a tsunami of tears or scream at the top of her lungs when things don't go her way. The development of the brain during adolescence allows us to feel our emotions and then express them in a socially appropriate fashion. To do this, the thinking and feeling parts of the brain must both undergo remodeling during the adolescent years.

Several recent brain imaging studies using MRI and fMRI indicate that key areas in the brain related to emotion are particularly reactive during adolescence. For instance, when processing emotions, teenagers exhibit greater increases in activity in the amygdala than children and adults do. The amygdala, a small almond-shaped structure located just in front of the hippocampus in the temporal lobes, with one on each side of the brain, plays a prominent role both in evoking emotional responses and in remembering what provoked those emotions—particularly negative ones.

The amygdala is responsible for the fear that many people feel when they see snakes, and for the anxiety caused by an algebra test, a blind date, or a job interview. The parts of the brain that process complex social information, including the frontal lobes, can easily activate the amygdala, allowing teens to obsess about why they aren't cuter, richer, or more popular, as well as to relive the time they got a vicious smackdown from the school bully. Unfortunately for teens, turning the amygdala off can be difficult. Greater activity in the amygdala during adolescence can periodically turn your teenager into an emotionally overwrought time bomb just waiting to explode. But it's not merely that he or she is more emotional. Rather, the adolescent brain has not yet developed the adult ability to balance emotional reactivity with cognitive regulation—the capacity for Captain Frontal Lobe to negotiate with Drama Queen Amygdala in order to avoid a meltdown.

The Reward System and the Pursuit of Pleasure

Until the 1950s, the neurological bases of pleasure were unknown. That changed when a psychological researcher named James Olds accidentally discovered a brain system that appeared to be responsible for mediating the feeling of pleasure. As a postdoctoral fellow in the laboratory of D. O. Hebb at McGill University in Toronto, Dr. Olds placed a small wire electrode into a specific area of a rat's brain to assess how the area contributed to behavior. Dr. Olds made a mistake during the surgery, and placed the tiny wire in the wrong brain region. Days later, while the rat walked around in an enclosure, Dr. Olds pushed a button and delivered a tiny electrical current that stimulated brain activity in the tissue around the tip of the electrode. To the amazement of both Hebb and Olds, that rat would repeat whatever it was doing at the time of the stimulation. If the rat was turning left when the stimulation came, it would keep turning left to try and recreate the highly rewarding pleasure in which it had just basked.

We now know that Dr. Olds had stumbled onto the brain circuitry involved in reinforcing, or rewarding, behaviors that are good for the survival of a species. Activating this circuitry has very powerful effects on behavior, because pleasure is so deeply rooted in the evolutionary quest for survival. If a living creature does something that activates the reward system, it will behave that way again. And again. And again. This is true whether the reward is a world-class slice of cheesecake, a

big hug from a friend, an ecstatic sexual experience, or a line
of cocaine.

The reward system is composed of two main parts: the
nucleus accumbens and the ventral tegmental area, both
located deep inside the brain. Neurons in the nucleus accumbens receive signals from cells in the ventral tegmental area
via the neurotransmitter chemical dopamine, and in turn,
distribute signals to a variety of other brain areas, including
the frontal lobes. In this way, the reward system is able to
engage far-flung brain regions and to influence behavior on a
large scale, and thereby help us learn about and remember the
reward and the behavior that caused the reward. Dopamine
is particularly involved in signaling that something important just happened and that the brain should pay attention
and learn about it. Endorphins, opiate-like compounds made
in the brain, are responsible for the resulting pleasure ride
itself. Importantly, the reward system is turned on not only
by rewards themselves but also by the expectation of future
rewards. And sometimes the expectation of reward can be a
more powerful motivator than the reward itself.

During adolescence, the reward system, like the amygdala,
is very easily excitable, particularly in anticipation of rewards.
In brain imaging experiments in which teenagers expect
rewards, they exhibit greater activity in the nucleus accumbens than children or adults. Teens' hyperreactive reward
systems motivate them to seek out objects or engage in behaviors that they expect to bring pleasure. But a hyperreactive
reward system can also lead to magical thinking, or what psychologists call "superstitious behavior." This is the tendency to
repeat a meaningless act just because it seems to be associated

with pleasure. Dr. Olds's rat was engaging in superstitious behavior when it kept turning left. Turning left hadn't actually made the rat feel good—it's just what the rat happened to be doing when its reward system got jolted by Dr. Olds's electrode. Similarly, an adolescent with a hyperreactive reward system may be more prone to repeat irrelevant or maladaptive behaviors simply because his reward system was easily activated when he engaged in those behaviors the first time. A stupid driving stunt or an in-class prank might get repeated simply because it once evoked a smile from a crush, hence triggering a dopamine explosion in the adolescent reward system.

The concentration of dopamine receptors in the nucleus accumbens—that is, the places on cells that cause them to activate when dopamine is around—is highest during adolescence, perhaps making that circuitry more responsive to the rewarding dopamine signals. As we'll discuss in more detail later, these changes in the reward system make substance abuse and dependence much more likely during adolescence because the brain is primed to react positively to anything that gives it pleasure, and to repeat such behaviors over and over.

It's easy to see how a hyperreactive reward system response, especially when combined with immature frontal lobes, can lead to a range of high-risk behaviors in teens. Psychologist Laurence Steinberg and his Temple University colleagues examined brain activity in teens, young adults, and adults while they played a driving game with or without a friend in the room. The friends did not actually interact with the participants; they were just in the room. The goal of the game was to reach the end of a driving course as quickly as possible. Participants had to decide whether to run yellow lights to get to the

monal master gland, the pituitary. Although the pituitary gland is part of the hormonal, or endocrine, system, it's so close to the hypothalamus that some axons from the hypothalamus reach down into the pituitary and have their way with it. This connection is a beautiful example of cross-talk between two of the body's most influential systems, the brain and the endocrine system.

The hypothalamus monitors the hormone content of the blood and sends signals to the various glands in the body, including the adrenals and the thyroid, stimulating them to increase or decrease their activity. It was long thought that the hormonal system functioned without much direction from the brain. But during the 1970s, scientists began to understand the role of the hypothalamus in controlling hormone levels, and it became clear that hormonal actions are in fact tied intimately to brain function.

The role of the hypothalamus is very broad. It regulates the physical changes that come with puberty and the onset of reproductive abilities, including the female menstrual cycle. It monitors and regulates insulin levels (which tell us how badly we want that bear claw in the bakery window). Thirst, energy level, the urge to snooze or party, and the desire to have sex are all regulated by the hypothalamus—a huge responsibility for a grape-sized bunch of cells.

Normally, in response to stressful stimuli or environments, the hypothalamus triggers a chain of events that releases a powerful stress hormone called cortisol from the adrenal glands. Cortisol affects a number of physiological systems, including gastric and kidney function and the immune system. It also contributes to the often uncomfortable feeling of stress. Puberty brings sharp increases in cortisol levels, which remain elevated into young adulthood. A little cortisol goes a long way, and can help the body prepare itself to deal with stressors and to form not-so-fond memories of stressful events. Too much cortisol, however, is associated with depression, the death of brain cells in the hippocampus, weakened immune activity, cardiovascular problems down the road, and a generally overwhelmed, exhausted, and freaked-out feeling. The stress response is not only stronger in adolescents than in adults but stays activated longer once initiated, explaining why an agitated teenager will often go ballistic when you suggest he calm down.

The Straight Dope on the Dopamine Connection

It's not just the form and shape of the brain that changes during adolescence. The levels of brain chemicals used for communication between cells and circuits also change. Dopamine levels, which we discussed earlier in the context of the reward system, are at their highest during adolescence. And they have a direct connection to the varied risk-taking behaviors teens engage in.

Certain groups of cells in the middle of the brain, which use the neurotransmitter dopamine, send their axons out to a variety of brain structures further forward and toward the top of the brain, including the frontal lobes. Dopamine stimulates the frontal lobes to pay attention by helping them to hone in on whatever action plan is currently under consideration and to ignore, momentarily, other competing actions. For instance, if the frontal lobes are working on an action plan for taking a pop quiz in math class, the dopamine signals help the frontal lobes to focus the whole brain on acing the test while keeping competing actions, like doodling or daydreaming, at bay.

Dopamine activity in these circuits increases significantly during the adolescent years, and diminishes with adulthood. Scientists theorize that heightened activity in these dopamine circuits places the brain in a state primarily motivated by looking for, going after, and consuming rewards, like a famished man with no self-control at an all-you-can-eat buffet. Food, sex, an adrenaline high from extreme sports, or a drug that produces pleasure are all potential rewards. This helps to explain why adolescents are so drawn to risk-taking when the risks seem to promise rewards, even if the risk might be deadly and the reward is no more than a giggle from another student.

Fully developed frontal lobes allow adults to do two things that adolescents find very difficult: delay gratification and inhibit impulsive reward-seeking, in actions such as not buying that overhyped, overpriced bathing suit you'll never wear but have to have instead of saving for insurance payments on your car. Of course, plenty of adults have trouble delaying gratification, too, but the combination of immature frontal lobes and ramped-up dopamine means more drive for reward plus less impulse control in adolescents, leading to more, and more dangerous, risk-taking. Fortunately, as each day passes, your teenager's brain will get better at delaying gratification and thinking about the future, while reducing the tendency toward rash reward-seeking.

THE TAKEAWAY

The changes taking place in a teenager's brain underlie the changes in behavior that help to move him or her into adulthood. Highly reactive emotional centers make adolescents overripe with impulses to explore, rebel, and take risks. These biological changes can drive a wedge between developing adolescents and the beleaguered adults around them. Development of sex-specific brain structures leads to increased motivation to attract potential sex partners and to work hard to gain their attention and acceptance. These changes serve as a perfect example of the intersection between puberty (physical and sexual development) and adolescence (social development). Remodeling of the frontal lobes during the adolescent years means grappling with short-sightedness and the overwhelming desire for instant gratification that sometimes allows emotions to control behavior. These changes can lead to stress and to explosions at home and school, but they also set the stage for getting teens out of the house and into the world to socialize and learn the broader rules of the culture; to become parents, partners, employees; to start a business; and to figure out who they want to be and what they want to do with their lives.

While all of these changes can serve valuable purposes, the modern world bombards rebellious, emotionally hyped-up, short-sighted teenagers with a stream of unhealthy, sometimes deadly options. This is why, sometimes, parents have to team up with their teen's developing frontal lobes to keep their teens safe.

In the chapters to come we will address issues that confront adolescents, their parents, and other involved adults. Most of them aren't new, because lots of the basic challenges faced by teenagers haven't changed that much in the last few decades. What is new is our ability to view those challenges through the lens of the latest research on brain development, and to adopt a new understanding of adolescence and how to navigate this developmental period with a maximum of happiness and a minimum of bloodshed. Understanding brain development in adolescence, and how it influences behavior, can help us guide teenagers in healthy ways and provide new opportunities for adults and teens to relate to one another without screaming, wailing, teeth-gnashing, or eye-rolling.

Knowing that teens are overrun with emotions, are ravenous for rewards, have hair-trigger stress responses, love to take risks, and have extreme difficulty using their frontal lobes to control emotions makes it easier to handle their season of discontent by finding and suggesting better ways to relax, enjoy, and ultimately thrive.

Chapter 2

MENTAL HEALTH

Your teenager hasn't bathed and has been wearing the same clothes for a week. He's just told you where you can stick the garbage that you asked him to take out. He spent the two hours before that silently sulking and ignoring everything you said, appearing to be a danger to himself and others. He's behind on his homework, hasn't finished his college applications, and all he can seem to think or talk about, when he talks at all, is his new favorite death metal band and the girl he's really, really, really into. Any of these behaviors could be a symptom of a severe mental disorder. Or it could just be another normal night in the life of a teenager who will go on to blossom and bloom and lead a happy, productive, fulfilled life.

So what does a mentally healthy teen look like? The answer might surprise you. The teen experience is like a bird leaving the nest in slow motion. Yes, we are sometimes tempted to give them a good hard shove out into the world. But our kids already come hardwired to give us a good hard shove of their own, and to spread their wings and begin their own slow, often less than graceful migration toward the exit sign. Extreme bouts of boredom, and endless whining about how much the rules and those who enforce them suck, all reflect the desperate desire to leave the nest. When teens tell us how different (and better) they'll be from us, and how differently (and better) they will treat their own kids, these are hopes for the future born from their drive to break free and create lives of their own. When they tell us our clothes are dorky, that the ways we sing, drive, eat, walk, and talk are an embarrassment, as painful as that may be, that's part of how our teenagers forge their own personalities and paths. They're testing their wings so they'll be ready to fly.

Does this mean that a teen who is polite and doesn't talk back to her parents is failing to prepare for the transition to the cold cruel world? Not necessarily. Sometimes the most cranky, cantankerous teen ends up a kidult, living in the basement way too long. Sometimes the teen who prefers to sit at home with her parents on a Saturday night soars into adulthood without looking back. However, for the typical teen, it is normal, natural, and even healthy to dislike parents and all they represent—at least for a time—in order to push away and begin heading for the door. These are all signposts that teens are on the right track, that they are experiencing normal adolescent development.

CIRCUIT CIRCUS

The teen brain undergoes rapid changes, particularly in the frontal lobes where the circuits are highly adaptable as they are molded into their mature, adult form. The plastic adolescent brain enables teens to flourish, from the ball field to the classroom to the social world, both real and cyber. However, the downside of this rapid change is that it creates the opportunity for brain development to go awry. Just as healthy experiences mold circuits in healthy, adaptive ways, unhealthy experiences mold the developing brain in unhealthy, maladaptive ways. Both types of training shape who we become as adults, which highlights the importance of creating healthy environments and appropriate contingency plans to route behavior and development down pathways that make optimal use of the malleable teen brain.

As they acquire an array of wondrous new skills and cognitive capabilities—from mastering electronic gadgets to navigating the dangerous world of dating—adolescents experience high stress. And high stress in teens can unmask and contribute to a variety of mental illnesses including anxiety and mood disorders, psychosis, eating disorders, and personality disorders. Because confusing and occasionally disturbing behavior is par for the course during the teen years, it is often hard to know when to be concerned about a teen and when to try to ride things out until they stabilize. The most common age for the onset of a mental health disorder is fourteen, according to the National Comorbidity Survey Replication study, which means that sometimes tumultuous adolescent behavior is not normal and points to something more serious.

Most parents have a keen sense of what is "normal" for their child. In general, abrupt, extreme, or long-lasting changes in mood and behavior should be taken seriously, in case they do not represent normal potholes in the road to autonomy. A normally bubbly and sociable teen who suddenly sulks in seclusion for more than a week or two may be drifting toward real depression. The chill skateboarder dude who becomes a snarky insomniac may be experiencing high levels of anxiety. There are as many examples as there are teens, but the abruptness, duration, and degree of change in personality and behavior are often the key to telling the difference between normal teen struggles and severe psychological problems. In this chapter, we'll explore how the most common disorders present themselves, what is short-circuiting inside the brain, and how to get effective treatment. But first, we're going to look at a mental health challenge that almost every teen faces: stress.

Stress

"I have no memory of being anywhere near as stressed about school as my daughter is. But she has packed so much into her schedule—soccer practice, violin lessons, her friends and her schoolwork—that she barely has time to breathe. I want to help her feel less stressed, but nothing I do seems to work."

Not all kids (or the adults around them) experience high levels of storm and stress during the teen years, but many do. And how they deal with stress during this period can greatly affect their quality of life and future ability to handle conflict, pressure, and difficulties. Stress is a normal consequence of clashes between teens' urge to fly free and the rules imposed upon them by parents, teachers, and other dastardly grown-ups. Stress also goes hand in hand with being challenged—in the classroom, sports field, on the job, in glee club, or on the school paper, in hanging out or hooking up. Much of this can be good stress, which helps teens develop coping skills, social flexibility, and the ability to play well with others that will prove useful in the adult world. But too much stress, or the wrong kind, can lead to depression, substance abuse, mood swings, anxiety, academic failure, family conflict, dangerous sexual behavior, extreme risk-taking, altered brain development, and even brain damage.

WHAT IS STRESS?

Stress is actually a combination of two things: 1) what causes us stress, or the stressor, and 2) our reaction to it, the stress response. The stressor can be anything—misplacing your keys, an impending math exam, the loss of a loved one, or squad car lights in the rearview mirror as you try to hide a beer under the seat. Stressors can actually be positive things, like a guitar solo at the school talent show, taking a free throw in the last seconds of a close basketball game, or applying to a college you'd really like to attend. Hans Selye, an early twentieth-century pioneer in stress research, distinguished between two kinds of stress: eustress, which encompasses stressors that can enhance life, such as hard work, exercise, and mastering a craft; and distress, which refers to stressors such as abuse, emotional deprivation, or being bullied, which can wear us down, making it difficult to enjoy life. We now use the terms "good stress" and "bad stress."

Regardless of whether a stressor causes good or bad stress, the body's initial reaction is the same: fight or flight. The stressor activates the sympathetic nervous system, which is responsible for mobilizing us to deal with stressors. Cells in the sympathetic nervous system get signals from the brain and send signals out from the spinal cord to muscles in order to dilate the pupils, jack up blood pressure, pump up muscles in our arms and legs, start us sweating, and get our hearts palpitating—all of which are our body's defense against threatening situations. The aim is to get ready for action—to prepare for battle or run from it.

At this initial, basic level, the body reacts to the stressor as if it were a threat. When a stressor is detected, a small area in the hypothalamus—the brain region that controls hormone levels in the body —discharges a chemical called corticotropin releasing hormone (CRH). CRH initiates a chain of events that causes the adrenal glands to release several crucial chemicals that prepare the body for acute crises, extreme danger, and life-or-death situations. The adrenal glands then release cortisol, the body's main stress hormone. Cortisol mobilizes the burning of stored fuel supplies to energize us, while reducing inflammation and pain (both of which hamper the ability to overcome life-threatening stressors). For example, a person involved in a car crash may be terribly injured but still be able to escape from the wreckage and even heroically rescue others. This is, in part, because the physiological stress response allows the body to easily access energy while blunting aches and pains long enough to take the steps needed to survive. It is a very primitive, animalistic, nonconscious, and effective adaptation. As long as the amount of cortisol in the bloodstream is not too high, it also promotes faster learning by the hippocampus, the brain region involved in memory formation. This enables us to remember situations clearly and learn from them, so as to be better prepared the next time the keys are lost or the car crashes. Of course, this learning/memory enhancement can have a terrible downside. Sometimes people remember traumatic experiences too well, and the memories become flashbacks which are intrusive and possibly debilitating. This hypermemory is likely one of the components of post-traumatic stress disorder (PTSD), and it can take time, and often professional assistance, to cope with such memories effectively.

The adrenal glands also release a compound called epinephrine, also known as adrenaline. Adrenaline is the body's caffeine. It speeds us up, increases heart rate, quickens breathing, causes thoughts to race, and may even create massive attacks of sweating and jitters.

Physical stress responses are rooted deeply in our biological past. From an evolutionary standpoint, all that matters is survival and procreation. Because our stress response is (or once was) so crucial to not getting eaten by a saber-toothed tiger or having our head smashed by a cudgel-wielding foe, our biological responses to stress are among the most powerful we experience. This is why extreme stressors such as one-time physical threats (a car racing by, a bomb going off, a bee about to sting) tend to evoke a jolting stress response. This is great from a survival perspective, but there's a catch: in the modern world, most people are not confronted with tiger fangs and cudgels. We may be biologically prepared to respond strongly to threats, but modern life rarely necessitates the full fight-or-flight response.

As we mature into adulthood and our frontal lobes become more adept at being effective CEOs, the occasionally crazy nature of our stress response becomes manageable. We learn that if we lose our phone, the world isn't going to end. But teens don't yet know how to manage stress, so they may experience overwhelming, out-of-control, and inappropriate stress responses. How they learn to cope has long-lasting repercussions, both positive and negative.

THE STRESS ROLLER COASTER

Stress can be a good thing when the stress response allows you to react appropriately to a stressor. In fact, mild stress actually improves motivation, concentration, and attention. If an impending exam causes no stress at all, it is less likely that you will study hard and do well. If you don't have a few butterflies before the big game, you may not play as well. On the other hand, too much stress or chronic stress can be debilitating. For example, if the looming exam produces an extreme stress response, you may find yourself immobilized at test time. If you puke your guts out before the big game and can't stop shaking, you're likely to be a miserable mess. Ideally, we would experience a stress response that turns on when faced with a genuine stressor and turns off once the stressor is gone. Too strong or too weak a response can lead to an overreaction when there is little danger, or an underreaction to a truly threatening situation.

Sometimes when teens are exposed to a high level of stress for a long period of time the stress response gets stuck in the "on" position even if the actual stressor itself is gone, as is the case with PTSD. When a person's stress response is chronically activated, whether due to sustained bullying or living with an abusive parent, it interferes with well-being rather than promoting survival. If the stress response is "on" long enough, it can actually seem to take over one's life. Again, adults generally have the experience and resources (including fully wired frontal lobes) to cope with chronic stress, whereas teens, because they are not as mature neurologically or emotionally, often react to stress in a more volatile way.

Chronic stress or regular acute stress can wreak havoc on the immune system, weakening the body's ability to protect and heal itself, and can also directly damage the brain. The hippocampus, which is crucial to the formation of new memories, is particularly susceptible to this sort of damage. Multiple studies have shown that a small amount of cortisol can help memory formation (as it does in the fight-or-flight response), while an overdose can actually kill the cells involved in encoding memories. The hippocampus in PTSD sufferers is often smaller than normal. But the relationship between memory and stress is complicated. Some traumatic memories may have been so effectively encoded by the brain that it flashes back to them over and over, while others completely vanish. For instance, the details of a car crash may be fuzzy or even blacked out, while the emotional memories are powerful and relentless. So even if a crash survivor doesn't remember a horn blowing during the wreck, his stress indicators may start ringing every time a car horn honks loudly. Part of the process of dealing with the fear and panic that may accompany traumatic memories is learning that you're safe in the present and the trauma is in the past. Hippocampal damage may impair this new learning, making the trauma even more difficult to overcome.

TEEN SUSCEPTIBILITY TO STRESS

Not getting the right dress for the prom may cause stress levels that would seem more appropriate to being on the deck of the sinking *Titanic*. Although there hasn't been much research comparing adolescent and adult stress responses, early studies suggest that teenagers react more strongly than adults to stressful stimuli, both behaviorally and physiologically, which could help explain going from prom ecstasy to despair in 2.4 seconds. Teens' immature frontal lobes make it hard to put stress in perspective. The adolescent brain's CEO is easily flustered.

Research has also shown that when adolescents are shown scary images, the amygdala—a brain area critically involved in the emotions of the stress response, particularly fear and anxiety—is turned on faster and harder than it is in children or adults exposed to the same things. Also, our ability to interpret facial expressions plays a big part in helping us figure out what (or who) should be feared, and teens are more likely to interpret facial expressions—particularly those of adults, and even more particularly those of their parents—as negative. It seems that teens are actually primed to feel stress in the presence of adults.

The hormonal response to stress is different in adolescents, too. Baseline levels of cortisol (the stress hormone) are similar in children and adults, but teenagers get a much bigger spike of cortisol when stressed. These shots of cortisol likely contribute to teens' freakouts in the face of stressors, even non-life-threatening ones such as homework overload or not getting to borrow the car. And once the stress response is turned on in an adolescent, the response is slow to be turned off, as is demonstrated by studies showing that stress-induced alterations in the skin's resistance to mild electric current (as in a lie detector test) take much longer to return to normal in teens than in adults.

Adults who chug double espressos may be able to relate to the exaggerated stress response experienced by teens. A recent study showed that the cortisol levels of adults who had consumed moderate to high doses of caffeine were more easily elevated. These adults also had exaggerated reactions to mildly stressful situations—just what would be expected from people with abnormally elevated cortisol levels, and people jacked up on caffeine.

Because of the changes in the stress response during adolescence, teens might actually be even more stressed out than they often look. They may spend large chunks of time in what pioneering endocrinologist Hans Selye called the "exhausted state"—a period of fatigue that often follows prolonged stress. And an exhausted state has consequences. Remember, high levels of cortisol can create memory impairment in people of any age, but in adult rats exposed to high levels of stress, the damage repairs itself in just two weeks. In adolescent rats exposed to the same stressors, damage to the hippocampus is still evident after a month (which for a young rat is a very long time). While we must interpret findings in animal models cautiously, these studies suggest that the adolescent brain may be more vulnerable to the long-term effects of chronic stress. This fits with what we know about the vulnerability of the adolescent brain to other insults, such as repeated exposure to alcohol and other drugs.

We also know that in adults, high levels of stress damage neurons in the frontal lobes. Luckily this seems to be reversible, at least in rats. The specific impact of stress on adolescent frontal lobe cells and circuits is not yet known, but new research suggests that because adolescents' more plastic frontal lobes are still developing, it is possible that high levels of stress could lead to more long-lasting changes, and possibly damage in frontal lobe circuits.

HELPING TEENS COPE WITH STRESS

Modern teens are bombarded by stress. Navigating the fierce jungle of high school, getting into absurdly competitive colleges, answering all those texts and instant messages—they get it from every direction. Stressed-out teens are more likely than adults to vent at those around them. When the prom dress crisis rears its ugly head, our lovely and composed teen is likely to lash out, often at innocent bystanders including moms, dads, siblings, and sometimes even dogs and cats. One simple strategy is to wait until the teen has calmed down before engaging him or her, particularly if the confrontation itself has the potential for fireworks. It's easy to react emotionally to your teen lashing out, but remember that teens' stress responses also last longer than yours, so a little extra time for decompression might be a very good thing. These biological realities do not excuse bad behavior, but they can put exaggerated reactions in perspective for both teens and the adults in their lives. Patience, empathy, and calm maturity from the grownup goes a long way toward preventing apocalyptic eruptions and long-festering feuds.

Exercise is another top stress reliever, though it works in a counterintuitive way. Vigorous exercise activates many of the physiological systems that are stimulated by stress—the heart rate increases, blood pressure rises, sweat glands start pumping. Both exercise and stress result in the activation of the sympathetic nervous system. But the magic of stress relief occurs after exercise, when the parasympathetic nervous system—a different branch of the nervous system—takes over to bring things back to normal. It's always active at a low level, but after the sympathetic nervous system pumps up our fight-or-flight response, the parasympathetic system relaxes the body, bringing it back to a state of equilibrium and relaxation. Since exercise isn't a threat, like a car accident or an assault, the body can let the parasympathetic activation calm and relieve stress after exercise. In other words, while going insane over an ill-fitting prom dress and running five miles may cause similar effects in the sympathetic nervous system, exercise doesn't leave you lugging around heavy emotional baggage—it actually gets rid of it.

Even small amounts of exercise can reduce the stress response in children and adolescents. In one study, kids aged ten to fourteen were put into two groups: one walked a mile, simulating a walk to school. The other sat quietly watching images of a typical suburban neighborhood, simulating riding a school bus. Next, the subjects took some mildly stressful paper-and-pencil tests. Those who walked had milder stress responses (smaller increases in blood pressure and heart rate) and reported fewer feelings of stress. So even though stress response is stronger in teens, it's been proven that at least in young teens these reactions can be powerfully diminished by exercise as simple as walking. The study also tells us that exercise does not completely eliminate the stress response, which is a good thing because mild stress can keep us sharp, focused, and motivated.

After-school athletic or recreational activities, or even an after-dinner walk around the block, can help a teen handle the stress of homework or the misery of not getting the prom dress of her dreams. And to decompress after those long evenings spent working on algebra problems or studying for a history exam, shooting hoops or a brisk bike ride are more effective than an X-Box encounter. Teens can also reduce stress by doing things that activate the parasympathetic nervous system directly and promote natural relaxation, such as meditation. One recent study found that twenty minutes of meditation per day (ten minutes at school and ten minutes at home) for three months lowered blood pressure and heart rate in middle school students. Those conducting the study taught students Transcendental Meditation (TM), a technique that involves repeating words or sounds, known as mantras, to help the brain let go of stressful thoughts and relax into a state of calm alertness. TM has been shown to reduce stress and increase calmness and self-reflection in middle school students. TM and other forms of meditation increase blood flow to the brain and are thought to actually improve the functioning of circuits in the frontal lobes. Studies have shown that meditation reduces the brain's response to physically painful stimuli, as well as to pictures or movie clips that evoke negative emotions. This suggests that the calming and stress-reducing effects that meditation has on the body may help to protect the brain against some of the damage that stress can cause.

Leading psychologists and neuroscientists in the US have recently begun using sophisticated brain imaging techniques to study the effects of integrative mind–body training (IMBT), a form of meditation based on traditional Chinese medicine. Some recent findings have been published in the highly prestigious *Proceedings of the National Academy of Sciences*. During training, coaches instruct people to focus on breathing, relaxing mental imagery, and maintaining a restful posture, in order to achieve a state of restful alertness.

One recent study focused on the anterior cingulate cortex, which is part of a network that is critical for the development of the brain's ability to monitor emotions and actions and to regulate behavior. Psychologists call this type of personal behavioral management "self-regulation." As we've discussed, much of the challenge of adolescent development revolves around regulating actions, emotions, and thinking. In the study, researchers found that meditation training increased the activity of the anterior cingulate cortex and improved self-regulation. And when meditation was practiced regularly, the actual physical connections between the anterior cingulate cortex and the rest of the brain were strengthened; the white matter tract which helps integrate these connections functioned more efficiently, allowing the anterior cingulate cortex to communicate more effectively with the other areas of the brain involved in self-regulation, such as the frontal lobes. So the CEO gets better information and makes decisions that are in the best interests of the corporation—in this case, your

allergic reactions, gastrointestinal discomfort, or pain. And, of course, feeling anxious is in itself a terrible stressor.

Anxiety is expressed differently at different ages. In elementary school, an anxious child may refuse to go to school, be terrified by thunder and lightning, or fret about life-threatening diseases, being kidnapped, or the ice caps melting. But in adolescence the worries turn to the most dangerous thing there is: other humans. Teens are often anxious about being shamed in front of peers, about not fitting in. While social anxiety is normal during the teen years, for some adolescents it crosses the line into social phobia, or social anxiety disorder, a fear of everyday social situations that can impair daily functioning to the point where, in extreme cases, people become terrified of even the most simple human interactions. Fears often revolve around being judged, embarrassed, or humiliated. Social phobia affects over 15 million people in the US. It is the third most common psychiatric disorder, behind depression and alcohol dependence, according to the National Comorbidity Survey Replication study. Sadly, it seems to attack early in life, often in adolescence. The peak age of onset is between ten and thirteen years of age, and it is estimated that 5 to 6 percent of teens between thirteen and eighteen experience symptoms of social anxiety disorder. If symptoms emerge for the first time after the age of twenty-five, they are almost always preceded by panic attacks or depression, which are less common when social anxiety disorder emerges during adolescence. So the typical onset in adolescents is different from that in adults.

Other anxiety disorders include separation anxiety disorder (SAD), generalized anxiety disorder (GAD), specific phobia, panic disorder, obsessive compulsive disorder (OCD), and post-traumatic stress disorder (PTSD). Each disorder has distinct symptoms, but people who experience any one of them are more at risk for others as well. While anxiety disorders come in several different forms, they share the same dysfunction in brain circuitry—namely, an amygdala that is in overdrive and hyperreactive to people, places, things, situations, or all of the above. Further, patients with an anxiety disorder are at increased risk for attention-deficit/hyperactivity disorder, and there is a strong link between anxiety disorders and depression. Therefore, it is critical to address anxiety disorders that emerge during adolescence aggressively and creatively in order to get maturation back on a healthy course.

Anxiety is often accompanied by physical complaints such as headaches, stomach cramps, vomiting, constipation or diarrhea, muscle tension, heart pounding, excessive sweating, hyperventilation, and insomnia. These physical symptoms cannot be dismissed as "all in your head," because anxiety makes them as real as real can be.

THE NEUROBIOLOGY OF ANXIETY

Even if we don't all develop full-blown anxiety disorders, almost everyone experiences anxiety. So scientists (and drug companies) have spent a lot of time trying to identify how the brain causes this debilitating feeling. The emergence of anxiety after puberty in girls, for example, has been the subject of many studies. We now know that stress causes the release of progesterone, a steroid that is derived from the female sex hormone, which is critical in the menstrual cycle. This steroid travels to the brain where it hooks up with the same receptors that are activated by alcohol and benzodiazepines like Valium. Before puberty, this steroid reduces anxiety, as you'd expect, because it activates receptors that produce feelings of calmness and relaxation. At puberty, there's a surge in the number of anxiety-increasing receptors. So the stress response that calmed anxiety at a younger age actually increases it after puberty. These changes in progesterone explain why girls tend to experience greater levels of anxiety, and why they are more susceptible to anxiety disorders during and after puberty.

Of course, boys experience anxiety as well. But, unlike progesterone in girls, there are no clear indications that specific chemical changes during puberty affect the likelihood or magnitude of anxiety in boys. It may be that rising testosterone levels in boys have a somewhat protective effect, making it less likely that they experience anxiety as girls do, or it may contribute to boys' general tendency to be less likely to discuss emotional distress. We're not certain, yet, what accounts for the sex difference in anxiety disorders.

TREATMENT OF ADOLESCENT ANXIETY DISORDERS

Freaking out over a prom dress is one thing, but if your teenager continually displays extreme anxiety, melting down over every little thing, it's time to take action. But what should you do? First, gather as much information as possible. If you can, watch how your teenager is interacting with peers, and check in with teachers, coaches, and other family members. In the end, though, your adolescent is the only one who'll be able to gauge his or her level of inner distress. It may be like pulling teeth with tweezers, but you need to try your best to get your teen to tell you what he or she is going through. Fortunately, anxiety is easier to spot than depression and other mental illnesses. Teens and adults tend to worry in the same ways, though often about different things. Once you scratch the surface of their protective shell, lots of teens are pretty good at describing when they feel worried or fearful. A good mental health professional experienced in adolescent anxiety disorders can make a proper diagnosis and suggest treatments.

Adolescent anxiety disorders are treated with both cognitive behavioral therapy (CBT) and medications. CBT is a treatment strategy that includes: (1) learning about the disorder; (2) becoming aware on a moment-by-moment basis of the body's reactions to stresses from the disorder; (3) developing methods of muscle relaxation, breathing, or creative visualization involving calming images that diminish the stress response; (4) cognitive restructuring, which means identifying negative thoughts and self-destructive speech and replacing them with more positive ones; (5) considering and practicing positive solutions for anticipated problems; and (6) a plan to prevent relapse. Every patient is different and it takes a skilled therapist to accomplish every goal, but when CBT is planned and carried out well, it is very effective.

CBT can also be applied to anxiety disorders in a manner similar to a vaccine. Patients are exposed to a small, safe dose so that they will be able to handle the invasive intruder, be it a germ or a paralyzing phobia. They are gradually exposed to the anxiety-inducing stimulus or situation in a controlled environment such as a doctor's office or a comfortable clinical setting. This way, the thing that causes the anxiety can be experienced while patients feel safe and relaxed, and in time, the feeling of fear is replaced by a relaxed or at least neutral feeling. This process, called systematic desensitization, has been used for decades to treat phobias and other disorders. When used within the CBT framework, it is a very good way to reduce anxiety.

We are also lucky to be living in the brave new world of computers. Nowadays, thanks to amazing adventures in brain imaging and virtual reality technology, your teenager can fall down an electronic rabbit hole into a computer-simulated environment that even ten years ago would have seemed like something out of a science fiction movie. In a therapeutic setting, your anxious adolescent might sport goggles with 3-D stereoscopic displays that change as he moves his head and even produce sound, smell, and touch sensations; in virtual reality, he or she is exposed to anxiety-inducing triggers in a precisely calibrated way while the clinician monitors that plastic teenage brain, paying special attention to those moments when the brain areas involved in stress start lighting up like Roman candles. By undergoing a gradually increasing intensity of the stimuli that cause the anxiety, the patient is able to gain mastery over the fear. This approach has been used successfully in the treatment of social anxiety, specific phobias (e.g. heights, spiders, snakes), and PTSD. This type of treatment is not yet available in your neighborhood doctor's office, but it's not so far off either. Many major medical centers are beginning to work with these technologies, and the virtual reality approach is becoming more accessible because of the availability of computers, software, and virtual reality peripherals, which in some cases exist as part of home gaming systems. We can envision a world where your teenager will be able to download this treatment with a smart phone.

We are also lucky to live in a time when medications are available to treat anxiety disorders in teens. But caution is key, because medications can cause both short-term and long-term side effects, depending on the drug, the dose, and the individual. And simply medicating your teenager will not solve all his or her problems. The most effective approach involves a combination of medication, meditation, and tools that teens can use on a daily basis to deal with thoughts and feelings that overwhelm them.

Although physicians have several medications at their disposal to treat anxiety disorders, the only drugs that have been proven effective for adolescent anxiety disorders in placebo-controlled trials are selective serotonin reuptake inhibitors (SSRIs) such as Prozac (fluoxetine), Zoloft (sertraline), and Paxil (paroxetine). In the largest study of its kind, researchers with the Child/Adolescent Anxiety Multimodal Study evaluated the effects of CBT, medication therapy, and the combination of the two on 488 subjects aged seven to seventeen who had been diagnosed with separation anxiety disorder, social phobia, or generalized anxiety disorder. Sixty percent of the participants responded well to CBT, 55 percent responded to the SSRI Zoloft, and 24 percent responded to placebo. The combination of CBT and Zoloft gave the best response rate, at 81 percent, making that the gold standard treatment for adolescent anxiety disorders.

Benzodiazepines such as Xanax (alprazolam), Klonopin (clonazepam), and Valium (diazepam) are another class of drugs widely used for the treatment of anxiety disorders in adults. Although they're sometimes prescribed for adolescents and children, there have not yet been solid, controlled studies to demonstrate their safety and effectiveness in those groups. These drugs carry a risk of dependence and, if they are stopped abruptly, can cause withdrawal symptoms such as poor sleep, gastrointestinal upset, high levels of anxiety, or even seizures. If they are prescribed, it should be for a limited time.

Buspar (buspirone) is a third type of drug that has been used to treat anxiety disorders in adults, but like the benzodiazepines it has not been proven effective in controlled studies of children or adolescents.

The best treatments are highly individualized and sometimes involve family or school participation as well as drugs and CBT. Twenty-four percent of teenagers given placebos told researchers they felt better. Twenty-four percent! This large number clearly suggests that for some teens, the simple belief that an effort is being made to help them, or perhaps just the passage of time, improves things. So, taking a teen's anxiety seriously by offering support, sympathy, and empathy can be a strong first step toward recovery. Also note that while medication is helpful, it works a lot better when you add CBT to the mix. Your family doctor or pediatrician may be able to prescribe the appropriate SSRI, but it's best to also consult a mental health professional well versed in CBT (a psychiatrist, psychologist, or clinical social worker) early in the treatment process. Your physician should be able to make a referral. The bottom line is that if adolescents suffering from anxiety disorders are treated appropriately, the disorder can be overcome.

Attention Deficit Hyperactivity Disorder

"My son does very well in school. He's on the honor roll, tutors other students, and is very attentive to getting his work done on time. But he also shows many of the symptoms of ADHD and they make him uncomfortable on a daily basis. I myself feel that I also am ADHD, but I had a much harder time in school. I want him to have relief, but I'm confused because he's such a good student."

Attention deficit hyperactivity disorder, or ADHD, is generally considered a learning deficit rather than a disorder of thinking or emotion, so most people don't think of it as a mental illness. However, because disorders of attention and concentration have such a powerful impact on the educational and social development of adolescents, and indeed on quality of life and prospects for immediate and long-term happiness, they also have long-ranging implications for mental health. As illustrated above, good students and high achievers aren't always free of ADHD's grip.

ADHD is one of the trickiest and yet most common disorders afflicting adolescents. Research suggests as many as one in ten school-aged children and adolescents are diagnosed with the condition. The constellation of behaviors associated with disordered attention is expressed differently in different people. One teen's unconventional style of working that feeds his art is another teen's spaced-out attention deficit disorder that stops him from becoming a great artist. But in general, people with ADHD tend to have symptoms that fall into one or more categories:

INATTENTION

- fails to pay attention to detail or makes careless mistakes
- has difficulty sustaining attention in tasks or play
- appears not to be listening when spoken to directly
- can't follow through on instructions
- has difficulty organizing tasks and activities
- is easily distracted by extraneous stimuli
- is often forgetful in daily activities

HYPERACTIVITY

- can't stop fidgeting or squirming
- when told to sit down, can't stop standing up
- has difficulty engaging in leisure activities quietly
- can't stop talking

IMPULSIVITY

- blurts out answers before questions are completed
- has difficulty awaiting turn
- often interrupts or intrudes on others

If you're an identical twin with ADHD, there's a 90 percent chance that your twin will have or develop it too. Among non-twin children who develop ADHD, between 10 and 35 percent have a parent or sibling with a history of ADHD. These findings suggest that while ADHD may not be 100 percent genetic in cause, heredity plays a strong role. So if you've got fidgeters and squirmers in your clan, keep an eye out for symptoms.

Attention is a cognitive ability and, to some degree, a learned skill. Now more than ever, at any given waking moment a teenager's brain is bombarded with stimulation: e-mails, texts, instant messages, parents, teachers, friends, coaches, boyfriends, girlfriends, television, YouTube clips, video games where you can be anything from a post-apocalyptic race car driver to a cold-blooded assassin. This stimulation comes streaming at us constantly through all five senses, and that's not even counting the information coming from our own internal cognitive and emotional states. To concentrate properly, the brain must act as a filter, choosing which bits of information and stimulation are important and which should be ignored.

Attention is like a flashlight with three different settings: high beam, low beam, and overdrive. High beam allows us to focus on specific stimuli or internal states. For instance, if your friend points and says, "Look at that cute puppy," you will most likely focus your attention on the cute puppy. Low beam allows us to focus more diffusely on a larger group of stimuli or internal states. If your friend asks you to look out the window of an airplane, you will most likely take in the whole panorama of landscape. The third setting, overdrive, allows us to focus on sometimes staggering amounts of information at once, whether it's navigating the chaos of heavy traffic or negotiating the combination of buttons and joystick movements required to play a video game. Overdrive is by far the most impressive setting; it's almost like having superpowers. But dividing attention is not easy. It takes a lot of frontal lobe control to get the various parts of the brain involved in processing divergent sensory information to work together. When the brain (specifically the frontal lobes) is not fully developed, this task can be even more daunting.

THE NEUROBIOLOGY OF ADHD

It's very difficult to learn if you can't pay attention. Attention is crucial to learning, and therefore a critical component of adolescent development as well as of success and happiness in the adult world. To pay attention, we have to isolate the thing we're trying to pay attention to from the vast array of stimuli bombarding the brain at any given moment. And we have to stop our brain from processing less useful information. The act of paying attention is largely a frontal-lobe-mediated process, and during adolescence our frontal lobe CEO hones its ability to direct attention, sustain it, and even split it when necessary. It seems reasonable that, as this development unfolds, our teenagers' frontal lobes will have good days and bad days. Our children often exhibit an amazing capacity one week to do all their homework, take out the garbage, and clean all the dishes without even being asked, and the next week to miss curfew, blow off choir practice, and forget to take out the garbage even after they've been reminded a thousand times. By the mid-teen years, however, the ability to concentrate and pay attention emerges strongly in most adolescents. When it doesn't, you should consider raising the concern with your family physician or school counselor.

Research suggests that the brain mechanisms that underlie ADHD involve faulty communication between the frontal lobes and an area of the brain called the striatum. The striatum plays critical roles in planning voluntary movements and processing time. Damage to this region is one cause of Parkinson's, in which people progressively lose the ability to voluntarily move their muscles. As captured in the book and movie *Awakenings*, which tells of the discovery of an effective treatment for Parkinson's, muscle reflexes remain intact but the ability to plan and execute a sequence of voluntary movements is compromised. The striatum and its neighboring structures (collectively called the basal ganglia) help the frontal lobes plan out a sequence of voluntary movements to be executed in a particular order to achieve a goal. This sequence may be used to do homework, take notes during a lecture, have a conversation, or just take out the garbage. If communication between the frontal lobes and striatum is compromised for some reason, the frontal lobes will not have the help they need to plan out the proper sequence of behaviors to accomplish the task. The main chemical messenger involved in communication between the frontal lobes and the striatum is dopamine. As we will see, increasing dopamine activity in the brain is the best strategy yet developed for normalizing communication between the frontal lobes and striatum and ameliorating the symptoms of ADHD.

TREATMENT OF ADHD

Even though we don't exactly understand what causes it, there are effective treatments for ADHD, both pharmaceutical and behavioral. A large study examining the effectiveness of various treatments suggests that medication plus behavioral therapy is superior to therapy alone.

Stimulants are the most commonly used class of drugs for treating ADHD. Drugs like Ritalin (methylphenidate) and Adderall (amphetamine plus dextroamphetamine) can work very well if prescribed properly after a thorough diagnosis. Between 75 and 90 percent of sufferers improve significantly with stimulants. But it's important that you and your physician carefully monitor your teen's use of medication like Ritalin. If, for example, the stimulants are taken before bedtime, they can cause problems with sleep. In addition, a number of teenagers deliberately misuse Ritalin and Adderall, and both have the potential to be addictive, as we will discuss in the chapter on drugs.

Stimulants increase levels of dopamine in the frontal lobes, which allows circuits within the frontal lobes, and between the frontal lobes and striatum, to regulate attention, control impulses, and guide focused behavior. ADHD symptoms tend to decrease as people age into their twenties, which also suggests that as the frontal lobes develop, the dopamine system there gets better at regulating those functions without outsourcing. But it's important to realize that although stimulants can help manage the symptoms of ADHD, there is no definitive cure.

Depression

"My son is so angry all the time. I rarely see a smile on his face. When I ask him if everything is okay, he either says

nothing or grunts something back. He is definitely not him-
self, but I don't know what's wrong or what to do!"

"Nobody likes me, everybody hates me, think I'll go and eat some worms." This children's ode to depression has been sung on playgrounds all over America for decades. Depression is a disease characterized by intense pessimism, lethargy, a sense that nothing can be done to change things, and lack of activity. It is often accompanied by a decrease in cognitive functions like memory formation and information processing speed. General memory function is suppressed in many depressed people. Sadly, and predictably, it's the memories of positive things that become hardest to access, whereas every little slight, every failure, every unachieved goal, is right at the mental fingertips of the depressed person.

One of the difficulties in understanding and dealing with depression is that each of us, from time to time, exhibits signs of being depressed. It's only natural that after a breakup, when the stock market crashes, or a loved one passes, we feel down in the dumps or that the universe is against us. We worry that things will never get better. What distinguishes normal periods of depression from the medical condition of depression is the length of time spent in the pit, whether we're able to climb out, and how fast we slide back into the storm of darkness. A clinically depressed person doesn't seem to be able to distinguish between the internal state of despair and the actual conditions in the outside world. While an otherwise healthy person might fall into a puddle of emotional pain that passes—time healing wounds as external events improve—a person with depression feels like she's drowning in despair even though she has a 4.3 GPA, is captain of the soccer team, and has a summer internship with a Supreme Court justice. No matter how many times people point out how great everything is and encourage her to just get over it, the depressed person can't separate the good from the bad.

A survey of 9,863 students in grades six, eight, and ten found that 25 percent of females and 10 percent of males reported depressive symptoms. In adolescents, depression may not manifest itself as might be expected—as feelings of deep sadness—but rather as irritability, boredom, or an inability to experience pleasure. Moodiness in adolescents is a time-honored tradition. But irascible rudeness and anger, chronic epic boredom, or deep dark funks lasting weeks at a time are not normal, especially if accompanied by changes in sleep, appetite, and energy. All adolescents tend to exhibit at least some of these symptoms from time to time, but the persistence and magnitude of the symptoms are what separate normal adolescent tumult from true depression.

THE NEUROBIOLOGY OF ADOLESCENT DEPRESSION

A clue to the biology of adolescent depression lies in puberty, the time at which hormonal changes begin. Prior to puberty, depression, anxiety disorders, and panic attacks are equally likely in boys and girls. After puberty, they are about twice as common in girls. This strongly suggests that sex hormones play a role in the emergence of these disorders even though they do not *cause* the disorders.

Mood is regulated by a dynamic interaction between the

frontal lobes (the prefrontal cortex specifically), amygdala, hippocampus, hypothalamus, and nucleus accumbens, all of which are ripe with hormone receptors and thus undergo robust changes at puberty. The hippocampus—which normally provides us with a healthy framework for grappling with stress—does not activate normally in depressed children and adolescents, hindering their ability to handle stress. The amygdala, which is responsible for assessing threats and filtering environmental stimuli, tends to be hyperactive in adolescents with depression. This could explain why your teenage daughter thinks you are launching the cruelest, most vicious attack in history when all you've done is ask her if she's doing okay. The hypothalamus, which regulates the four F's of behavior—fighting, fleeing, feeding, and mating—releases hormones that cause testosterone, estrogen, cortisol, and adrenaline to be released, all of which affect mood. The nucleus accumbens, the heart of the brain's reward system, responds to dopamine. Because dopamine levels are lower throughout the brain during adolescence, there is less dopamine for the nucleus accumbens to respond to, and therefore any mood may be darker during this time. Dopamine levels in the prefrontal cortex increase throughout adolescence, enhancing connections between all regions and therefore strengthening the ability to handle stress, which otherwise brings on depression and anxiety. But until the prefrontal cortex has fully matured and these four regions are working together like a well-oiled unit, stressors can cause mood changes, including depression, in ways that are particular to adolescents.

TREATMENT FOR DEPRESSION

Although highly effective treatments are available, most depressed adolescents don't get the treatment they need. Depressed teens often go untreated because they don't want to ask for help, they think it won't make a difference if they do, or they don't know how or whom to ask. Sometimes parents and other adults assume that sullen irritability and bitter moodiness, which can be symptoms of depression, are simply signs of teenagers being teenagers. This is why it's important to pay attention to teenagers' moods and feelings, and to ask questions with sympathetic persistence when a down period goes on for longer than a few days.

If you suspect that your teen is depressed, your family doctor or pediatrician is a good place to start. Primary care physicians can offer effective treatment in the form of antidepressants. However, family doctors may not have specific training in mental health disorders, so we recommend that you also consult a psychiatrist or psychologist. It's important to take action and to give as much accurate information as possible, because depressive symptoms can accompany other serious mental health problems such as psychosis, bipolar disorder, suicide attempts, or substance abuse. A family history of any of these disorders can markedly change the treatment plan for a teen who may be presenting for the first time with depressive symptoms.

As with anxiety, psychotherapy and medication have been shown to be effective in treating adolescent depression. The type of psychotherapy that has been studied most thoroughly and that has proven to work best is, again, CBT. And once again, medications of choice are selective serotonin reuptake inhibitors (SSRIs). SSRIs are effective in about 60 percent of subjects. An older class of medications, the tricyclic antidepressants, are not a good option for adolescents because they have not been shown to be better than placebo, and the risk of a fatal overdose is much greater than with SSRIs.

SSRIs work on synapses, the junctions between neurons in the brain. Neurons communicate when chemicals are released from one neuron and float across a tiny gap called the synaptic cleft to bind like a key in a lock to receptors on a receiving neuron. There are many different types of neurotransmitters floating across synaptic clefts. The ones typically targeted by psychiatric medicines—including antidepressants—include dopamine, norepinephrine, and serotonin. Normally, neurotransmitter molecules bind with receptors on the receiving neuron for a short time, and then are released and snatched back up into the neuron from which they came so they can be used again, in the brain's private recycling system. In a depressed brain, too few neurotransmitter molecules are released—or perhaps they are being snatched back up into the releasing neuron too quickly. SSRIs work by helping the transmitter remain in the synaptic cleft so that it can bind to the receptors of the receiving neuron for more time.

There are currently nine different SSRIs on the market, and forty different brand names. Studies have shown all of them to be effective in general, but some work better than others for different people. This is where a skilled psychiatrist comes in; sometimes finding the right drug and the right dose involves close monitoring and some trial and error. SSRIs are safe and effective for many adolescents with depression, but they can involve risk. The most common side effects, which are often mild and temporary, include gastrointestinal symptoms, headache, agitation, and sleep disturbances. A more rare but extremely serious side effect is an increase in suicidal thoughts. A review by the FDA of nearly 2,200 teens and children treated with SSRIs found that although no suicides occurred as a result of taking the medications, 4 percent of teens taking them experienced suicidal thinking or behavior—about twice the rate amongst those taking placebo pills. Because of this, the FDA has issued a "black box" warning (its strongest warning for prescription drug labeling) for use of all antidepressants in the pediatric (i.e. non-adult) population.

Why might there be a link between antidepressant use and suicidal thoughts in kids? The answer has to do with the complicated changes in neural circuits and within brain cells themselves that occur as the patient begins taking antidepressants. Most antidepressants take a month or more of daily use to kick in, because it takes consistent exposure to the drug for those brain changes to occur. Once they do occur, there are often noticeable improvements in mood. Clearly, the therapeutic changes the brain goes through on these drugs do not depend solely on immediately available levels of neurotransmitters like serotonin. If they did, the drugs would work immediately. Early in treatment, your depressed teen may find herself with more mental energy but no real improvement in her emotionally depressed state. It could be that the enhanced cognitive activity, when combined with poor emotional functioning, makes it easier for depressed patients to get pulled into the quicksand of suicidal thoughts. The hope is that as the medication eventually takes full effect, the improving emotional state catches up with the enhanced mental activity and the individual will be out of this danger quickly.

While the black box warning points to a real and important risk, the downside is that the warning may scare away physicians, teens, and their families from a treatment that will very likely be safe and effective. A good psychiatrist will closely monitor any adolescent patient on SSRIs for continued depression, agitation, or suicidal thoughts. This is especially important during the first four weeks of treatment. But when used properly, these drugs, along with proper psychological therapy, can immensely help your teen overcome the crippling effects of depression.

As parents and caregivers, it's important to acknowledge the emotional struggles that teens face. Their feelings should be considered on their own terms, and not in comparison to others. Offer the simple comfort of understanding. No adult can know exactly how a depressed teen feels, but adults can show that they believe what the teen feels is real and painful, that the rough time will pass, and that they will not be driven away by the bout of depression. When a caring adult can assure a teen that help is available and that they will find it together, a potentially life-saving alliance is formed.

Suicide

"My daughter has now alluded to suicide enough times to make me deeply concerned that it's something she's actually contemplating. My daughter's best friend also men-

tioned to me that my daughter had said something about
not wanting to be part of this world anymore. She has had
periods of being very down before, but ending her life has
never been something she's talked about. I'm desperate
and scared."

Suicide is the third leading cause of death for people age twelve to twenty-four. Boys are four times more likely than girls to kill themselves, though girls are more likely to make an attempt. According to the Centers for Disease Control, 17 percent of female and 11 percent of male high school students contemplated suicide seriously in the year before they were surveyed, 13 percent of females and 9 percent of males made a plan for suicide, and 8 percent of females and 5 percent of males attempted suicide. Sadly, suicide is impossible to predict. But several factors are known to increase the risk, such as substance abuse, access to firearms, psychosis, and a family history of suicide attempts. If your teen talks about suicide, starts throwing away important belongings, complains of being a bad person, or drops hints like "You won't have to worry about me much longer," take it seriously and seek outside help immediately.

The undeveloped nature of teens' frontal lobes and other brain regions interferes with their ability to process stress and other emotions. Urges bubbling to the surface build up sufficient pressure to swamp the cognitive control centers and lead teens to act in unhealthy ways. For some kids, this pressure generates unruly behavior. For others, it generates self-destructive behavior. An amygdala sent into hyperdrive because of a humiliation in front of the whole school—or the whole world, if it's online—may generate so much worry, fear, and self-loathing that the future seems unbearable and death seems a reasonable choice to the overwhelmed frontal lobes.

During adolescence, the future is measured in weeks, days, and nanoseconds rather than months, years, and decades. Ask a fifteen-year-old about his plans for the future and he'll probably tell you about the party that night or the game coming up the following week. As adults, we (hopefully) recognize that heartbreak, rejection, harassment, and conflict with others can sting, wound, and sometimes scar at the deepest level, but that somehow, some way, we'll get by with a little help from our friends. This isn't as easy for adolescents, who lack the cognitive maturity to think far into the future, particularly if their entire life experience has made them feel as though things will never ever get better. As irrational a choice as suicide might seem to most adults, sometimes it's the only action that makes sense to a desperate kid.

Anorexia Nervosa

"My daughter was always a picky eater, but now she pushes her food around her plate, comes up with excuses about why she's not going to eat, is obsessed with her appearance, and is so thin that she appears ill. My wife and I have tried every parenting trick in the book to get her to eat, but these seem more appropriate for young children. There are other girls in her school that seem to be going

> *though the same thing, but we are wary of bringing it up*
> *with their parents. Our daughter's weight has crossed the*
> *line and something needs to be done."*

Anorexia nervosa can be extremely dangerous. Sufferers are obsessed with food and body weight, which leads them to eat less and less and less. Some exercise excessively in their relentless pursuit of thinness. The most striking, disturbing, and incomprehensible psychological feature of anorexia nervosa is the distorted view that sufferers have of their own bodies. They see themselves as fat though a mirror clearly reveals that they are emaciated.

Anorexia nervosa occurs nine times as often in females as in males, and in about 0.6 percent of the population. Forty percent of all cases occur between the ages of fifteen and nineteen, and 0.56 percent of fifteen-to-twenty-four-year-old women with anorexia nervosa die each year from complications associated with the condition. This means that anorexia nervosa has one of the highest mortality rates among psychiatric disorders. A young woman with anorexia nervosa is twelve times more likely to die than a woman of the same age without the disease. The good news is that many people who suffer from anorexia will ultimately recover.

THE NEUROBIOLOGY OF ANOREXIA NERVOSA

As with anxiety and depression, the fact that females are more likely to experience anorexia nervosa gives us a clue to its biological basis, although the exact biological mechanisms of the illness remain unknown. One theory is that it results from a pathological response to the female hormone estrogen, which normally causes mild suppression of appetite. At least one study has reported an abnormal type of estrogen receptor in patients with anorexia nervosa, suggesting that estrogen's normal tendency to repress hunger is magnified in anorexics. But further research is needed before scientists can begin work on estrogen-related treatments.

Another possibility is that self-induced starvation itself triggers brain changes that reduce the urge to eat. This theory emerged from the highly controversial 1944–45 Minnesota Starvation Experiment, which was designed to assess the effects of famine and guide Allied relief efforts for the millions of people in Europe and Asia suffering severe food shortages as a result of the Second World War. Working with the Civilian Public Service and the Selective Service System, the investigators recruited thirty-six conscientious objectors who were committed enough to the relief effort to submit themselves to a yearlong study of starvation. The study was divided into four phases: (1) a twelve-week control phase, during which the subjects' physiological and psychological baselines were established; (2) a twenty-four-week semi-starvation phase, during which they lost about 25 percent of their pre-starvation weight; (3) a twelve-week phase in which they were divided into four groups, each receiving a different recovery diet; and (4) an eight-week unrestricted diet with ongoing behavioral and physical assessments. During the semi-starvation phase the subjects developed many of the psychological and behavioral features seen in anorexia nervosa, such as social withdrawal, decrease in metabolic rate, irritability, decline in social functioning, and depression, suggesting a vicious cycle in which starvation actually motivates a person to continue to refuse food.

However, biology is only part of the story with anorexia nervosa. We live in a culture that indoctrinates girls from a very early age with the idea that thin is beautiful, that "you can never be too thin." Supermodels, princesses, pop stars, movie stars, and gymnasts—people who often rigorously watch their weight—are some of the most prominent role models for girls in our society. Boys are not immune to these cultural influences; certain activities, such as wrestling, demand that boys pay an inordinate amount of attention to what they weigh, sometimes prompting them to lose drastic amounts of weight in ridiculously short periods of time.

Although there is still a lot to learn about these factors, which vary widely across cultures and even across social groups within cultures, we do know that the risk of anorexia nervosa is higher in environments and professions that place a high value on thinness. Let's face it, if you go to a private school in Beverly Hills, you're more likely to obsess about your weight than if you live in an average American town. If your teen is interested in modeling, dancing, acting, or sports like wrestling or gymnastics that emphasize weight control, make sure you talk to him or her about the pressures related to eating and about how to maintain a balanced and healthy perspective on eating and body image. Coaches and trainers can have a positive influence as long as they focus on the overall health of the teen rather than on encouraging unhealthy body weights for the sake of performance or appearance.

If your teenager becomes overly concerned with eating or thinness after getting involved with a new crew or starting a new activity, it's time for you to step in and express concern. While anorexia nervosa has become a disturbingly common phenomenon, fortunately family doctors, pediatricians, school counselors, coaches, and others have become far more aware of the warning signs and are now better equipped to help teens recover.

TREATMENT OF ANOREXIA NERVOSA

Because there are so many physical causes of weight loss, the initial evaluation for anorexia nervosa is more medically intensive than for the other disorders we've discussed. Brain tumors or other cancers, infections, neurodegenerative diseases, and a host of hormonal conditions may cause symptoms that can be confused with anorexia nervosa. A thorough medical workup including laboratory tests is usually a good idea.

Once a diagnosis is made, the first priority is to get the person back to a healthy weight, because while the disorder might have psychological roots, the physical effects can be fatal. This may require hospitalization with close monitoring of caloric intake and constant supervision to prevent self-induced vomiting. In extreme cases, where death is imminent, doctors may use a feeding tube to ensure that the patient isn't starving herself to death. Once the patient has achieved a healthy weight, the focus of treatment switches from medical stability to individual, family, and group therapy that will identify the issues that led to the disorder and help prevent relapse. Therapy may be valuable in the initial stages of treatment as well, but it's important to tend to the patient's physical well-being first.

Because depression and/or anxiety often accompany anorexia nervosa, the medications discussed above may be prescribed. However, it should be noted that antidepressant and anti-anxiety medications alone have not been shown to be very effective in treating the core symptoms of anorexia nervosa.

Bulimia Nervosa

"We started noticing that our daughter was going to the bathroom immediately after every meal like clockwork. Then I discovered diuretics in her backpack. When I asked her what was up, she became infuriated that I had gone through her bag and refused to answer. I was briefly bulimic as a teenager, so I know what this is. But I'm at a complete loss for how to deal with the issue with my own child."

Unlike anorexia, in which a person's body weight can be grotesquely subnormal, bulimics often have normal body weight. Rather than refusing to eat, bulimics binge on food and then make themselves vomit or take large doses of laxatives to avoid absorbing all of the calories. Like anorexia, bulimia is more common among people involved in activities where thinness is prized, such as gymnastics and modeling. However, in the modern world, where images of stick-thin, airbrushed starlets assault teenagers every time they boot up a computer, turn on a TV, or look at a magazine cover, it's easy to imagine how much pressure all developing young people must feel to look perfect and how easy it is to slide into bingeing and purging. Like anorexia, bulimia is much more common in females than males. Bulimics are significantly more likely than non-bulimics to have depression or anxiety disorders and to abuse substances.

Obviously, without time for digestion, the body can't absorb what it needs from food, let alone any medications. A less obvious but major risk of repeated bulimic bingeing and purging comes from bathing the mouth and throat in highly toxic stomach acids, which eat away at tooth enamel and create painful and dangerous ulcers in the esophagus. When laxatives are used, healthy bacterial flora in the gut is swept away, negatively affecting digestion and the absorption of important nutrients.

THE NEUROBIOLOGY OF BULIMIA

As with other disorders that emerge during adolescence, it turns out that there is a strong genetic component to bulimia. Researchers at the Virginia Institute for Psychiatric and Behavioral Genetics studied nearly two thousand pairs of twins and found that if one twin suffered from bulimia, there was a 60 to 80 percent chance that the other twin would suffer from it as well. There is also evidence linking a specific chromosomal region to families with a history of bulimia. So, bulimia seems to involve both nature and nurture.

TREATMENT OF BULIMIA

Anywhere from 25 to 75 percent of bulimics suffer from depression. In recent clinical studies, antidepressants were found to cut bingeing and purging associated with bulimia by more than 50 percent. The effectiveness of antidepressants for bulimia is roughly equivalent to the benefits of cognitive behavioral therapy. It makes sense to utilize a combination of the two approaches.

Schizophrenia

"I am a single parent to my son. His mother and I got divorced after she had a psychotic break when my son was just two years old. I have been monitoring my son very closely because I know that schizophrenia has strong genetic links. And I've started to notice some strange behavior, including paranoia. Some of his friends have somewhat similar behavior, so I'm confused about whether he's just being a teenager or if he may be exhibiting early signs of this terrifying disease."

Schizophrenia is a serious illness that causes disordered thinking and unusual behavior. The disordered thinking (or psychosis) may take the form of hallucinations, which are sights or sounds that aren't there, such as voices that order the listener to do things. Schizophrenics may also experience delusions, which are fixed false beliefs, such as the idea that the world is out to get them or that they're receiving coded messages from a god or aliens.

Adolescent schizophrenia is often associated with a childhood history of delays in motor or language development as well as mild cognitive and social impairment. The more obvious psychotic symptoms are often preceded by a "prodromal phase" of odd beliefs. These can include paranoia, mistrust of others, or magical thinking which may begin days or weeks before the emergence of more severe psychotic symptoms. Social withdrawal, prolonged foul moods, decline in personal hygiene, and poor decision-making are all possible indicators of schizophrenia. Of course, those behaviors are also just another day in the life of John and Jane Q. Teenager, so it's important not to jump to conclusions. But when odd or very uncharacteristic behavior lasts more than a few days or is accompanied by unusual thinking or ideas that seem out of sync with reality, a mental health professional should be consulted.

Here are some of the most common symptoms of schizophrenia:

- **Delusions:** False beliefs held in the face of substantial evidence to the contrary
  - of grandeur: belief that one is an important character, such as Napoleon or Christ
  - of persecution: belief that others are plotting against you
  - of reference: belief that someone or something is delivering personal messages to you
- **Hallucinations:** Sensory phenomena not corroborated by others, usually auditory
- **Incoherent thoughts:** Breakdown in normal thinking that often involves jumping wildly from one idea to another
- **Odd behavior:** Long periods without movement, poor hygiene, odd speech patterns, and the like
  - Echolalia: Repeating things that other people say

- Word salad: Stringing partial sentences together in an odd, often loosely associated, way
- Neologisms: Making up words

THE NEUROBIOLOGY OF ADOLESCENT SCHIZOPHRENIA

About one in one hundred people will develop schizophrenia, and if you are related to a schizophrenic, you have a greater chance of developing the disorder yourself. If an identical twin has schizophrenia, there's a 50 percent chance that the other twin will have it; if a non-identical twin or sibling has schizophrenia, the risk is about 10 percent. So, schizophrenia is highly but not completely heritable, meaning that its roots are probably biological as opposed to social or cultural. But despite the fact that those genes are present from birth, the symptoms of schizophrenia usually don't manifest until the late teens or early twenties.

The emerging science of adolescent brain development offers important clues as to what is happening in the brain when the symptoms are unleashed, and how can they be controlled. Pathological brain changes observed in schizophrenics—including decreased cortical gray matter, changes in brain activity during sleep, and changes in frontal lobe activity—are exaggerations of the changes going on in all adolescent brains. This is not to imply that schizophrenia is caused by normal maturation running amok. Subtle differences in brain structure during childhood suggest that it is more complicated. But the number of pathologic findings suggests a developmental aspect to the disease. This is currently the subject of intensive research, which may soon substantially alter both the understanding and treatment of schizophrenia.

TREATMENT OF SCHIZOPHRENIA

It's particularly difficult to diagnose schizophrenia in teenagers, in part because their "typical" behavior may be anxious, moody, irrational, sad, manic, sullen, and distracted. Many conditions other than schizophrenia lead to psychotic symptoms during adolescence, including severe depression, bipolar disorder, exposure to environmental toxins, head injuries or concussions, and substance abuse. Each one requires a different treatment, so it's important to consult an expert for a thorough diagnostic evaluation. This will entail a careful physical and neurologic examination, gathering information from multiple sources like parents and teachers, and a meticulous review of the patient's medical and family history.

Schizophrenia can affect nearly every sphere of a teen's life, from having lunch in the cafeteria to getting along with parents and siblings at home, to hanging out with friends, to figuring out what the heck to do with the rest of one's life. Traditional CBT can be beneficial for schizophrenia, and intelligent, well-informed support from friends, family, coaches, teachers, and counselors may also be helpful. But because of its biological basis, schizophrenia is almost always managed with judicious use of medication and sometimes hospitalization.

The first-line drugs for adolescent schizophrenia are antipsychotics. Although these medicines are effective in reducing symptoms and helping teenagers function on a daily basis, the side effects tend to be more severe than those of SSRIs and anti-anxiety drugs. They can include substantial weight gain (adding stress to the life of a teen already trying to cope with a serious psychiatric disorder), metabolic problems, and even movement disorders including akathisia, a feeling of inner restlessness and the urge to be in motion. People with akathisia fidget, rock from foot to foot, or pace. Another movement disorder side effect is extrapyramidal syndrome, which can result in involuntary muscle movements or spasms, often in the face or neck. These side effects can be scary and should be a serious concern when treating schizophrenia, but it's important to emphasize that, because schizophrenia can lead people to behave in dangerous and self-destructive ways, it's far better to treat the disease and manage the side effects than to let teens go without treatment. As with SSRIs, some antipsychotic medications work better than others and have different side effects in different individuals. As with all the medications we've discussed, it's very important to have a psychiatrist with particular expertise in schizophrenia and/or adolescence prescribing and monitoring the use of these drugs.

SEEKING HELP

Because there are not yet any laboratory or imaging tests that can definitively confirm a diagnosis of schizophrenia, depression, or other psychiatric illness in either teens or adults, the diagnosis depends on tracking a pattern of symptoms and behaviors. Pathological patterns that are hard to pick up in the early stages of illness will become more obvious as the illness

What Is Normal?

How do you distinguish between your teen blowing off steam and the onset of a mental disorder? There are no rigid standards, because every teen is different and every behavior has a different context. The following list gives examples of behavior that may indicate a need to seek professional mental health services:

- Statements or actions of harming self or others
- Psychosis (e.g., hallucinations, delusions, breakdown of normal thinking)
- Substance abuse
- Prolonged negative mood and attitude, especially if accompanied by marked changes in sleep, appetite, or energy level
- Inability to cope with day-to-day problems or activities
- Evidence of an eating disorder
- Marked deterioration in academic performance
- Sharp increase in sexual behavior or sexual acting out
- Consistent aggression or violation of the rights of others, fighting, truancy, theft, or vandalism

worsens. This is just one reason why it's almost impossible for sufferers to self-diagnose, and why parents, teachers, coaches, other adults, and even friends can be extremely helpful. Often, these people know what normal is for a teen and can identify when something's wrong. The other side of the coin is that those closest to a sufferer might be taken aback, emotionally wounded, or mortally offended by his or her behavior and therefore see a disorder when the adolescent is simply being an average teenager. While parental intuition should be taken seriously, it's critical to have an objective professional assess your teen. When parents and experts work together closely, it's often possible to identify problems early on, when treatments can be most helpful.

If you're not sure where to go for help, talk to someone you trust who has experience in mental health. This can be anyone from the school nurse to your pediatrician to a friend who has dealt with a similar situation. Ask advice on where to seek treatment. If there's a university medical center nearby, its department of psychiatry or psychology may offer a private and/or sliding-scale fee clinic with affordable diagnostic and treatment options. You can also contact the National Alliance on Mental Illness (NAMI) through their website, nami.org. And in times of crisis, the emergency room doctor at a hospital should be able to provide at least temporary help for a mental health problem, and will be able to tell you where and how to get further help.

People and organizations that are likely to provide advice and referrals are:

- Family doctors
- Mental health specialists, such as psychiatrists, psychologists, social workers, or mental health counselors
- Community mental health centers
- Hospital psychiatry departments and outpatient clinics

- State hospital outpatient clinics
- Social service agencies

At the stroke of midnight on a teen's eighteenth birthday he or she becomes legally independent in ways that can be terrifying for parents—especially for parents of teens with mental health issues. For example, once your teen turns eighteen a doctor cannot discuss his or her condition with you without permission, which means that the doctor may not be allowed to keep you in the loop on the treatment plan, compliance with medication, checking into or out of a hospital, etc. It is crucial to build open communication with your teen early and often, and then rely on that openness after age eighteen: discuss the coming independence in the months leading up to it (ability to manage medication, etc.), and what you hope—hope, not expect—communication will be like. Express pride and confidence in the teen's emerging adulthood and the judgment and responsibility that will emerge with it, but let him know that you are there, that just because a person turns eighteen, graduates from college, gets a job, or has a family does not mean that they must do everything on their own. Offer to be a resource—an authoritative, but not authoritarian resource. Hopefully this will reassure your teen that you trust his or her ability to be a thriving, self-sufficient adult, but that you will always be there to help if needed.

Chapter 3

FOOD

It's often great theater to watch teenagers eat. Whether they're gorging themselves on inhuman amounts of ridiculous or frankly nauseating combinations of food, or shoving their meal around the plate as if it's going to bite them instead of the other way around, witnessing an adolescent strapping on the feed can run the gamut from astonishing to terrifying.

Obviously the machine that is the body must be fueled. Because teenage brains are working overtime, they need the energy that food provides to keep them moving. The trick is to get them to eat the right foods to keep their energy levels up. When a soda and a candy bar are easy to grab—which they always are—chances are that these are the foods many teens will choose. And the food choices teens make during adolescence will affect the rest of their lives. As we all know, it's difficult to make eating and lifestyle changes during adulthood. So we must help our teens establish healthy eating and physical activity habits while their brains are elastic and primed to learn. This is now more important than ever, as today's teens are the heaviest in history.

On the flip side, many girls become super-conscious of their bodies during the adolescent years and make ill-informed choices as to what to eat and what not to eat. A small percentage of these girls will start curbing their diet in life-threatening ways.

Whether your teen is eating too much or too little, or simply making poor choices about what to put into his or her body, you'll want to provide information and guidance as to why eating in a healthy way is vital to a healthy brain.

Food for Thought

The brain weighs three pounds, making up only 2 percent of a typical teenage body weight, yet it sucks up 20 percent of the energy the body generates. Every time a thought flashes in your mind and a neuron communicates with its neighbors, energy is consumed and more energy is needed to replace the spent fuel. With its complicated networks of electrically active neurons, the brain is a ravenous, energy-hungry beast.

Because your teenager's brain is trying out and discarding so many new connections, it's not very energy-efficient. As we approach adolescence, the volume of gray matter in the frontal lobes and other areas of the cerebral cortex increases, preparing the brain for the structural transformations that will soon occur. In order to meet the demands of all of that new gray matter, the brain craves more energy. As brain circuits become more refined and precise and the volume of gray matter decreases, the total energy demands of the brain decrease. The adult brain is like a focused flashlight compared to the adolescent's floodlamp. Efficient brain circuits allow adults to complete tasks faster and with less energy.

We eat to provide our bodies with energy. The energy bonds between the molecules found in food are used to generate the fuel utilized by every cell in the body. In addition to vitamins and minerals, we extract three basic components from the foods we eat: carbohydrates, fats, and proteins. Each plays an important role in brain function.

Carbohydrates consist of simple sugars (such as sucrose found in table sugar), and complex sugars (such as starches found in vegetables). Complex sugars are composed of chains of simple sugars. Carbohydrates are a good source of quick energy because they can be converted rapidly into glucose, the body's preferred energy source.

Fats come in two forms: unsaturated and saturated. Unsaturated fats are extracted from nuts, fish, olives, and vegetables and generally are healthier than saturated fats, which come from meats and dairy products. Fats can be converted to glucose, used to make hormones, or stored for fuel. They play a role in the formation of membranes around cells, including those around neurons and glial cells (the brain cells that support the work of neurons and promote their ability to communicate with one another). Indeed, because the brain is packed with so many neurons and glial cells and their membranes contain fatty molecules, the brain itself is more than 50 percent fat.

Proteins are made up of amino acids, which are used to build new cells and repair damaged ones. Amino acids are also used to build neurotransmitters, such as serotonin and dopamine (two of the neurotransmitters most closely linked to mood regulation and feelings of pleasure). In addition, amino acids make up enzymes in the brain that play a critical role in breaking down molecules when they are no longer needed and putting together new ones.

There is no bodily process that does not depend upon nutrition. Because of its rate of development, particularly in the frontal lobes and related circuits, the adolescent brain requires all of the energy and metabolic resources provided by good and balanced nutrition, and suffers when it doesn't get what it needs.

HOW THE BRAIN CONTROLS EATING

The brain mechanisms that regulate eating and body weight are only partially under our conscious control. The hypothalamus controls the balance between the amount of food energy we take in and the amount of food energy we use or store. It also monitors the levels of circulating hormones related to eating and energy storage, making us feel more or less hungry, and slowing or quickening our metabolism accordingly. The hypothalamus is constantly engaged in a delicate balancing act: determining whether we're hungry and how hungry we are, and then signaling us to stop eating once we've had enough.

While activity in the hypothalamus is beyond our conscious control, thanks to the decision-making power of our frontal lobes, we can choose when to eat and when to stop. We can also influence how much stored fuel we burn by deciding how often and how hard we exercise. Neuroimaging stud-

ies show that the frontal lobes become more active after eating, while the hypothalamus becomes less active. The extra
activity in the frontal lobes probably indicates that we're consciously trying to stop ourselves from eating more, though the
science isn't completely settled on this issue. The hypothalamus functions differently in obese people, taking longer to
respond to glucose intake, and brain imaging studies suggest
that their prefrontal cortex has to work much harder to suppress the urge to eat.

THE REWARDS OF EATING

Eating a delicious dessert makes most people feel almost high.
This is not an accident. In fact, some of the brain areas involved
in the enjoyment and reinforcement of eating, including the
reward system, are also involved in seeking and using drugs.

People respond to food as a reward in two phases. First
is anticipation. Imagine staring down at your favorite dessert, be it banana cream pie or a chocolate sundae. Anticipat-
ing the pleasure of that first bite is a pleasure in and of itself.
Just as when a junkie goes through his ritual for shooting up,
the sight and smell of food triggers increases in dopamine
released in the heart of the reward pathway in the brain.
When we finally slide that delicious first bite into our mouths,
more dopamine streams into this same pathway, resulting in a
heightened feeling of happiness and well-being. Together, the
effects of anticipation and consumption on the reward system
make eating a highly satisfying experience. Unfortunately, we
humans are prone to choose foods that are damaging to our
health, like those high in fats and sugars, because they power-

fully activate the reward system in the brain. This presents a special challenge to the highly reactive teen reward system.

The Trouble with Sugar

"We don't keep soda in the house, but my son drinks at least a couple Cokes a day either at school or at after-school activities. He doesn't do any sports and I see he's starting to gain weight. Would eliminating these sodas really make a difference weight-wise? I don't want to make a big deal about it unless it's really necessary."

Although the brain and the rest of the body use glucose as a primary source of energy, this does not mean that eating a lot of sugar is a good idea. In the past, sugar was typically obtained by eating foods that were naturally sweet, such as fruits and vegetables. Fruits contain sugar, though not in nearly as high a concentration as the foods with added sugar or sugar substitutes that line the shelves of supermarkets today. The extra sugar found in cookies, chips, and other processed snacks may come from sucrose found in sugar cane and sugar beets, or fructose from fruits and corn. Dozens of natural and artificial sugar substitutes such as agave, aspartame, saccharin, and sucralose are also available, and many taste far sweeter than natural sugar. Because of its importance to bodily function, it makes sense that humans would have evolved to worship at the altar of sugar. It feeds our reward system and gives us a temporary jolt of pleasure and reinforcement. So what's wrong with eating sugar? Nothing, as long as it's in moderation.

The United States Department of Agriculture (USDA) advises adults who eat a 2,000-calorie diet to limit sugar consumption to about 10 teaspoons of added sugar (above and beyond those that occur naturally in foods like fruits) per day. A teenage male who follows a healthy diet can eat about 18 teaspoons of added sugar, according to USDA. That said, the average sugar intake of US teenage males is a whopping 34 teaspoons per day. It's easy to understand how this overload occurs; just one can of Coca-Cola contains 9.29 teaspoons of sugar. And there are high levels of sugar in everything from hot dogs and other processed meats to breads and breakfast cereals, to "health food" snacks like granola bars, so chances are that one added candy bar would put most Americans way over the recommended limit.

The changes in the brain and the rest of the body that occur when sugar is consumed help explain why too much is unhealthy. When a person consumes a high dose of sugar, such as a can of Coca-Cola, the pancreas releases a large amount of the hormone insulin in order to move the sugar out of the blood and into the cells where it can be used as fuel. Insulin also converts any extra sugar into glycogen in the liver, where it is stored. When a big load of sugar bombs into the bloodstream, maybe after that Snickers/Coke combo, so much insulin is released and it works so quickly to move the sugar out of the blood and into the tissues that the blood sugar level actually decreases very rapidly. As blood sugar levels drop, it becomes harder to pay attention and to keep information active in short-term memory. The drop in blood sugar also triggers the adrenal glands to release adrenaline and the stress hormone cortisol. Cortisol causes the liver to convert the stored glycogen back into glucose, which temporarily brings blood sugar levels back up again. This is a dangerous roller coaster ride, and repeating it too frequently or with very large sugar highs and lows can result in insulin resistance and the onset of type 2 diabetes. As the cycle repeats, the body learns to ignore the insulin signal set off by massive sugar intake, and the insulin can't get sugar into cells or store fuel as glycogen. The excess sugar gets stored as fat.

Rapid rises and falls in blood sugar levels drain the brain. After a sugary snack, neurons get all fueled up. As mentioned above, this causes a temporary improvement in concentration and memory. However, because neurons can't store glucose for later use, the subsequent insulin spike and fall in blood sugar levels leaves neurons starved for fuel. This drop in the brain's glucose levels creates the opposite of the initial, brief increase in concentration and memory: feelings of inattentiveness, fatigue, weakness, and in some cases nervousness.

High-fructose corn syrup, or "corn sugar" as it's called by the companies that produce it, also poses problems for the brain. The hormone ghrelin, which is secreted by the stomach, tells the brain we need food. Another hormone, leptin, released primarily by fat cells, tells the brain we've eaten enough. The sugar in natural foods suppresses ghrelin release, decreasing the hunger signal, and increases release of leptin, signalling us to stop eating. Studies have shown that high-fructose corn syrup doesn't sufficiently suppress the release of ghrelin, nor does it increase leptin levels as much as the sugar naturally found in foods does. So foods containing high-fructose corn syrup make the brain feel less full than foods containing other forms of sugar. This, of course, leads to overeating.

Ultimately, it's best to fuel the body with natural sugars. Complex carbohydrates, such as starch from vegetables, are long chains of sugar molecules. Because they need to be broken down to produce simple sugars, they cause slower rises in blood sugar levels and are less likely to lead to insulin resistance and its health consequences.

Finally, extra sugar also means extra calories, which will cause weight gain unless exercise is increased dramatically. In fact, research indicates that there's a clear relationship between the amount of sugar kids consume and the likelihood that they'll become overweight or obese.

The Trouble with Caffeine

"As a coffee drinker, I didn't think I'd be affected by drinking one of those extra caffeinated drinks that my son and all his friends drink. But after drinking just one at night, I felt uncomfortably hyped up and for the first time was concerned about my son's regular use of these drinks. I don't know if it was the combination of caffeine and sugar that made it so potent. But it was powerful."

In the Broadway musical *How to Succeed in Business Without Really Trying*, office employees lament, in song and dance, that if they can't take their coffee break, something inside them dies. Caffeine is a habit-forming drug. If you don't believe us, ask the millions of Americans who feel like they have cotton candy for brains if they don't get their coffee fix, and experience nasty headaches for a day or two if they try to kick the habit. When used in moderation, however, caffeine makes us think and feel better. In fact, it's the most widely used recreational drug on the planet and is found in more and more foods and beverages, from iced tea to Red Bull. By mildly activating the fight-or-flight response, caffeine increases energy and vigilance. For adults, the caffeine in two cups of coffee significantly increases activity in the frontal lobes, which temporarily helps us pay attention and learn. Caffeine's influence on the reward system also gives us a sense of pleasure and well-being. When a person drinks more than a few cups of coffee, however, he or she will likely feel jumpy or jittery, and have difficulty paying attention.

There's an important difference between how teens and adults take in caffeine. Children and adolescents typically prefer to get their caffeine in sugary beverages, which has contributed to the wild popularity of energy drinks like the sugar- and caffeine-saturated Red Bull. Both sugar and caffeine activate the reward pathway, so these drinks pack a potent one-two punch which neither sugar nor caffeine alone can replicate. The hyperreactive reward system in the adolescent brain may make this combination even more attractive.

Adolescents aged twelve to seventeen who consume caffeine take in on average the equivalent of one cup of coffee—about half the amount that is consumed daily by caffeine-drinking adults. Although more and more teenagers are consuming more and more caffeine, its effects on the function and development of the teen brain are not yet fully understood. What is clear is that caffeine consumption late in the day, or excessive caffeine consumption at any time of day, leads to trouble falling and staying asleep. Because many adolescents struggle

to sleep long and well enough, it's important that they understand the negative consequences of caffeine misuse and adjust
their consumption accordingly. Many adolescents struggle
with anxiety and restlessness, both of which can be exacerbated by even moderate doses of caffeine. Research also indicates that withdrawal from caffeine produces the same pattern
of effects (headache, drowsiness, and fatigue) in adolescents as
adults, and those effects can have a terrible impact on mood
and school performance.

The possible long-term effects of caffeine consumption during adolescence have not been extensively addressed, but there
is one study in rats that raises a cautionary flag. Animals
treated with caffeine during adolescence were more emotionally reactive and behaved more impulsively than animals who
spent their adolescence caffeine-free. The caffeinated rats

The Caffeine Nicotine Blues

For teenagers, caffeine and nicotine stroll hand in hand.
Adolescents who drink more than four cups of coffee (or
the caffeine equivalent) are more likely to be smokers than
those who take in less caffeine. Nicotine and caffeine have
similar effects in the brain, increasing arousal and produc-
ing pleasure through activation of the reward system. As
with sugar and caffeine, the combination of the two seems
to produce more reinforcement than either produces alone.
There is evidence that caffeine might actually prime the
brain so that it's more responsive to the rewarding effects
of various drugs, including nicotine.

also had heavier adrenal glands, suggesting that their level of stress response may have been chronically elevated by prolonged caffeine exposure (see chapter 2 for a full explanation of the stress response).

How Many Calories Do Adolescents Need?

"My daughter consumes twice the amount of calories recommended for someone her age. She is also considered overweight for her age. However, she is a very serious athlete, has no fat that I can see (she's all muscle), and she looks healthy as can be. Something is off here!"

The amount of energy in the foods we eat is measured in calories. In the US, the word "calorie" on a food label actually means "kilocalorie," or 1,000 calories. So, we use a capital "C" to differentiate between the little calorie and the big Calorie (1000 calories). Depending upon how much a person weighs, how old they are, how much they exercise, what medications they take, and other factors, the body requires somewhere between 2000 and 3000 Calories to charge through a typical day. When more Calories are consumed than are needed, body weight goes up, and when more Calories are burned than are taken in, stored fuel is burned and body weight goes down. The USDA suggests that adolescent girls need around 2200 Calories per day, while adolescent boys need around 2800 Calories per day. But relying too heavily on average numbers can be misleading. For example, a teenage wrestler will probably burn lots more Calories than the head of the chess club, and the chess fanatic might actually gain weight while consuming the recommended number of Calories.

These days, rather than using just body weight to assess whether one is eating too much or too little, the Centers for Disease Control recommend using a measure called body mass index, or BMI. BMI is calculated according to height and weight, and the formula is adjusted for age and sex. Because body fat changes markedly throughout adolescence and is different for boys and girls, the age-adjusted BMI is particularly useful. And because excess levels of body fat represent a health risk on their own, BMI is more valuable than weight as an indicator of health. If you want to know whether your teen's BMI is within the normal range, the CDC offers a calculator at cdc.gov.

When Does Overweight Become Obese?

> *"My husband and I are both overweight. And now my son and my daughter have tipped the scales in the wrong direction. At my daughter's last doctor's visit, her pediatrician said she is at risk for developing diabetes. It feels like just yesterday she was a skinny kid. I'm mortified that I have let this happen. And I know I've been a terrible role model."*

Between the late 1970s and 2008, the rates of obesity among adolescents aged twelve to nineteen went from 5 percent to 18 percent. Obesity is most likely to emerge during childhood or adolescence, and those who are obese between the ages of ten and thirteen have an 80 percent chance of being obese as adults. An overweight teenager is set up for a lifetime of health problems.

Where are the lines between Rubenesque, overweight, and obese? Using the age-adjusted BMI, those scoring in the eighty-fifth to the ninety-fifth percentile for their age group are overweight. Those scoring above the ninety-fifth percentile are obese. If a fourteen-year-old boy is 5 feet 8 inches tall and weighs 160 pounds, giving a BMI of 24, he is overweight. If he weighs 185 pounds, his BMI is 27 and he is obese. Obesity interferes with healthy adolescent development by straining the cardiovascular system, liver, and pancreas, and by contributing to psychological difficulties and physical ailments. Risk factors for obesity in adolescence include:

- Overeating or binge eating
- Lack of exercise
- Family history of obesity
- Medical conditions that slow down metabolism (e.g., thyroid problems) or prevent adequate exercise (e.g., injuries)
- Medications (e.g., steroids and some psychiatric medications)
- Stressful life events (e.g., divorce, death of a loved one, abuse)
- Interpersonal conflicts with family or peers

Obesity during adolescence can lead to:

- Depression
- Anxiety

- Obsessive compulsive disorder
- Low self-esteem
- Increased risk of heart disease
- High blood pressure
- Diabetes
- Breathing problems
- Trouble sleeping

Obesity is not just about weighing more than a certain number of pounds. Being severely overweight not only puts adolescents at risk for a variety of negative outcomes in both the short and the long term, it also reduces life span. So why don't we all, both adolescents and adults, simply eat and exercise enough to keep our bodies going and our weight at a reasonable level? The answer is simple: eating feels good. That is why learning to regulate food intake and to exercise properly is part of a healthy foundation for adulthood.

EARLY ONSET PUBERTY

Hormonal changes that jump-start sexual maturation are often influenced by the amount of fat stored in the body. There are good reasons for this. The adult female body requires enough stored nutrients to sustain a healthy pregnancy. Studies show that the brain monitors levels of leptin, the hormone released by fat cells, to estimate how much stored energy the female has available. When an appropriate level of leptin is reached, the hypothalamus swings into action and puberty begins. The massive numbers of overweight and obese young people may help explain why children are entering puberty earlier than they did a century ago.

Much of the research on the age of puberty onset has focused on girls. For example, in the US, the age at which girls begin menstruating has decreased from roughly fourteen to twelve over the last hundred years. In countries where girls have less body fat than in America, menstruation starts later. When young girls from other countries move to the US and adopt American eating habits, their periods begin earlier than expected. Early puberty not only brings psychological effects, but also means that your child is maturing sexually long before she is mentally prepared to manage the urges and responsibilities that accompany an adult body, and may well feel awkward and out of place with other children of her age. Additionally, early onset puberty brings an increased risk of breast cancer. A new 2012 study indicates that boys in the US are entering puberty earlier as well.

Programs aimed at reducing obesity also delay the onset of puberty, and therefore help bring bodily and psychological changes more into line. Researchers at the Harvard School of Public Health selected 508 girls aged ten to thirteen from ten different schools and monitored them over two years. Half of the schools utilized a health education curriculum called Planet Health, which aims to reduce obesity by increasing the consumption of vegetables and physical activity, while decreasing TV time and high-fat foods. Girls at the schools that followed the program gained less weight, had less body fat, and began puberty later than girls at the schools without the program.

The Planet Health program clearly changed behavior, and those behavioral changes profoundly influenced development. We emphasize this because many people, some scientists included, assert that educational programs alone cannot change health-related behavior in a meaningful way. We could not disagree more strongly. As the Harvard study shows, well-crafted and thoughtfully applied educational and behavioral approaches can significantly change teens' eating and exercising habits, thus improving their health and well-being.

Anorexia and Bulimia

"My daughter goes to a private school in New York City where eating disorders seem to be as common as the common cold. I thought my daughter was very healthy around her food choices, but now that she's fifteen, I'm seeing a new level of consciousness about her body and what she's eating. I want her to understand that an eating disorder is not cool. I've seen friends go through both anorexia and bulimia and I will do anything to prevent my daughter from going through the pain of these disorders."

On the other end of the spectrum from obesity are anorexia and bulimia. We wrote about eating disorders from a medical and psychological perspective in Chapter 2, focusing heavily on diagnosis and treatment. But eating disorders are deeply tied to how we think and feel about food, so it's important to offer some complementary information here.

It's estimated that more than half of American girls are dissatisfied with their bodies by the age of thirteen. By the time they reach seventeen, nearly four out of five will have at some point felt unhappy about how they look. All these girls don't have eating disorders, but clearly a large percentage of today's teens (and especially girls) struggle with being comfortable in their own skin. The desire to look a certain way may simply reflect the typical adolescent urge to fit in, but it's important to distinguish that urge from the early signs of potentially dangerous eating disorders and to be certain that teens have a realistic perspective on how much and what kinds of eating are normal and healthy.

Anorexia can cause significant, potentially permanent damage to the brain. Unlike other organs in the body, which can use alternatives to glucose for fuel, the brain is highly dependent on glucose to support normal function—especially during the energy-intensive teen years. Choking the brain off from the glucose it needs impedes growth, development, and many functions. It can even lead to cell death. Over time, the brain shrinks and the psychological health of the starving person suffers. The body literally devours itself in an effort to keep fueling the brain. It can be difficult for a healthy person to concentrate after skipping just one meal. Imagine the toll it would take on your teenager's physical performance and emotional well-being if she skipped meal after meal, or ate only tiny meals for days and weeks on end.

Unlike teens with anorexia, whose body weights can be painfully, dangerously, and obviously low, bulimics often have normal body weight. Yet bulimia is also associated with brain atrophy, or shrinkage, though less so than anorexia. The volumes of gray matter and white matter in the brain decrease as a result of both disorders, suggesting that the damage is not restricted to particular areas. Although brain shrinkage is obviously dangerous and reflects a serious insult to the body, research suggests that much of this damage might be reparable. Still, it is possible that compromising the brain during such a significant developmental period might seriously retard its development.

The lack of nutrition in teens suffering from eating disorders can lead to widespread and dangerous changes in neurotransmitter systems in the brain, including decreased levels of serotonin and dopamine. Boosting the availability of neurotransmitters involved in mood regulation through the use of antidepressants can help, which suggests that deficiencies in those transmitters may be one of the causes of the disorder. But the picture is complicated; it may also be that nutritional deficiencies caused neurotransmitter levels to fall.

What Should Teens Eat?

"We have a very healthy household where everyone eats tons of veggies, fruits, and whole grains, and very little sugar, processed foods, or foods with additives or preservatives. My son tells me about what his friends eat and I'm shocked! But what's funny is they all love eating at our house. So I don't think teens inherently want to eat badly. I just think those are the choices presented to them, which is very sad."

Because the body uses food to build brain cells and neurotransmitters, it makes sense that the foods we eat have an impact on how we think, perform, and feel. While it's unlikely that mood or performance will be significantly affected by a single meal (though a really great one can certainly make you happy), giving the brain access over time to the right building blocks for cellular function can have a positive lasting effect.

Amino acids from the protein we eat can be used to assemble enzymes. Enzymes are designed both to put small molecules together into bigger ones and to take big molecules apart. In this way the body constructs the proteins in our hair, the hormones involved in puberty, and the neurotransmitters our neurons use to communicate. Enzymes also break down, or metabolize, alcohol and other drugs and recycle the components of dead cells. All these activities promote brain circuit activity. It follows that the amount of protein we eat influences the amount and types of neurotransmitters produced in our brains, and therefore affects mood, sleep, and cognitive or physical performance.

Given that so much of the brain is made up of fat—not just cell membranes for holding receptors in place, but also myelin sheaths for speeding communication between cells—it makes sense that the brain would also utilize fats from your diet. There are many types of fat that we encounter in food or that are made naturally by our bodies, but one—omega-3 fatty acids—is critical for the brain to function at its best. Unfortunately, the body cannot make omega-3 fatty acids; you have to ingest them. Fish and some other seafood, along with oils from nuts, contain high levels of omega-3s. Research shows that consuming these fatty acids, either in food or in supplement form, improves not just bodily health but emotional health (hence the recent prevalence of omega-3 and fish oil pills on the shelves of health food and nutritional stores).

Although the science is not yet settled, some research suggests that omega-3s help with depression—whether it results from major depressive disorder or bipolar disorder—and may also be beneficial to people with ADHD. It's still unclear how this form of fat helps fight depression, but, given the role that omega-3 fatty acids play in building the membranes around neurons and glial cells, it's possible that they boost the overall efficiency with which brain cells communicate, thus allowing circuits to function better even under adverse conditions.

And then there's breakfast. It's no accident that breakfast is known as the most important meal of the day. While a good overall daily nutrition schedule is essential, a nutritious breakfast helps the brain rise to the challenges of the day. As discussed, the brain requires glucose in order to function, and when glucose levels are low, the brain suffers. Eating a balanced and healthy breakfast leads to an increase in blood sugar levels and provides the brain with the fuel it needs to pay attention in class and create memories of what's being learned. It's critical that the breakfast consist of foods that don't simply cause a blood sugar spike followed by a crash, because the crash may be worse for performance than having no breakfast at all. The trick is to avoid simple sugars, such as those found in many breakfast cereals, donuts, Pop-Tarts, and other fast but unhealthy foods. Eggs are a great source of protein, as are whole grain cereals, pancakes made with whole wheat flour, or fruit smoothies made without added sugar. A good breakfast makes for a better mood, improves classroom behavior and attentiveness, and helps your teen get better grades. But just because breakfast is important doesn't mean teens should eat it twice! Sometimes children and adolescents take advantage of school breakfast programs and end up eating breakfast at home *and* at school. Those extra calories will have a negative impact on weight and health. Encourage teens to pack a healthy morning snack so they won't feel the need to take advantage of a second breakfast.

Snooze Your Way to Thin

Two recent studies show one very natural behavior that teens can engage in to improve their diets: sleep!

A Case Western Reserve University study shows that adolescents who sleep an average of eight or more hours on weekdays consume a less fatty diet than those who sleep less than eight hours. Another small but potentially important study recently published in the *Annals of Internal Medicine,* a journal of the American College of Physicians, showed that dieters who slept for 8.5 hours per night lost 55 percent more body fat than dieters who slept only 5.5 hours per night. The participants who slept less felt hungrier throughout the study than those who got more sleep, suggesting that the lack of sleep may have affected the hormone ghrelin, which regulates feelings of hunger and causes the retention of body fat. The study concluded that limited sleep while dieting diminishes the effectiveness of the diet. Though their study was conducted on adults, we can assume that similar processes would be in play in teens who are trying to diet.

TRAIN THE BRAIN TO EAT IN HEALTHY WAYS

Decisions about drug use, studying, friends, and diet are regulated in large part by the frontal lobes. As we know, the frontal lobes are undergoing great changes during the adolescent years. How might those changes influence dietary choices? Dr. William Kilgore and Dr. Deborah Yurgelun-Todd of Harvard Medical Center recently compared the brains of female subjects aged nine to fifteen with adult subjects as they viewed pictures of various foods, including some that were particularly high-calorie (cheeseburgers, French fries, ice cream sundaes). The amount of activation in the brain structures involved in emotion and memory were similar in both age groups. However, the amount of activation in the frontal lobes increased with age, suggesting that as our brains develop during adolescence, we begin to think harder about the foods we see rather than simply reacting to them emotionally. Kids rely on emotion and memory rather than on reason when it comes to food. Then, as they enter their teen years, they use their maturing frontal lobes to make more intelligent, on-the-spot judgment calls about healthy food choices.

Experience plays a big role in how the brain operates when it makes dietary choices. Children and adolescents learn what, when, and how much to eat chiefly from those around them. Obviously, this presents both opportunities and pitfalls. If kids get accustomed to eating healthy foods at young ages, building strong associations between healthy foods and good emotions and memories, the habit of eating healthy things can stick through adolescence and beyond. Having fruits, vegetables, and other healthy foods available on a daily basis—and keeping highly caloric and sugary foods out of the house—makes a huge difference.

Sometimes the trick to getting a teen thinking about diet can be to provide information in a context that interests them, such as athletic performance, making friends, or getting better grades. This may mean adults have to make some changes, too. Adults who lead by example, showing teens how to eat healthily, influence their kids' eating choices for the better—today, tomorrow, and for the rest of their lives.

Chapter 4

SLEEP

The average adolescent leads a life that would exhaust a Fortune 500 CEO. Between classes, sports, extracurricular activities, driving lessons, parties, SATs, homework, gabbing, texting, posting videos, teens can end up burning several candles at both ends. Sleep often gets shoved aside because there are literally not enough hours in a day. This is bad news for teenagers, as restful sleep is vital for maintaining good health in general and good brain function in particular. Failure to get enough sleep makes for moody (or rather, moodier!) teens and can result in family conflict, bad grades, and failure on the playing field.

Science has answered a lot of questions about the workings of sleep, but the ultimate purpose of sleep remains a mystery. Some scientists believe we sleep at night to conserve energy. We humans come from a long line of daytime creatures. Before the advent of electricity, there really wasn't much we could accomplish at night, so why not sleep and save our energy for more productive daytime hours? Others believe that sleep is a time when our stifled emotional urges are expressed in dreams. And still others think that sleep allows us to create memories—that information acquired during the day is consolidated, or transferred, into long-term storage while we snooze, making sleep essential to learning.

Even though the jury is still out regarding why we really need to sleep in the first place, it's been proven that a regular sleep/wake cycle improves attention and mood, as well as academic, athletic, and social performance. Sleep is a time of repair for the brain. We all know what a toll a few nights of poor sleep can take. And too little sleep for too long not only makes us cranky and impatient, but also impairs our ability to think clearly and make good decisions. Even one night of poor sleep can be dangerous.

Unfortunately, adolescence is a time when basic sleep patterns are in a state of flux. Compared to children and adults, teens exhibit a natural tendency to stay up later and sleep in longer. Many teens sleep in a restless way, tossing and turning, and they wake up frequently. And one thing is true for the majority of teens: they don't sleep enough.

This Is Your Brain on Sleep

Why is sleep so important, and why do we humans need to get so much of it? Until the early twentieth century, scientists believed that sleep was what happened when the brain received too little stimulation. Turn off the lights, lie in a quiet room, and sleep happens. Obviously, it's not quite that easy. And it turns out that sleep is actually an *active* process. Falling asleep and waking up are triggered by changes in brain function, rather than simply being induced by changes in the light.

Sleep is divided into four stages based on the brain's patterns of electrical activity. A normal night's sleep involves switching between these stages, and repeating the cycle several times. When we are awake but relaxed, brain waves exhibit a fast pace with a low amplitude. These are known as alpha waves and they reflect lots of activity across multiple brain circuits, as might be expected when one is planning the day and trying to figure out how to get the new boy's attention while studying for an upcoming exam. As we relax and drift off to sleep, brain waves shift into a slower-paced, higher-amplitude form called theta waves. Theta waves indicate that brain cells are synchronizing with one another, firing in linked patterns, and reducing the random chatter in the brain.

The transition from alpha waves to theta waves is called stage N1 sleep. During this transition from wakefulness to sleep, sudden twitches and jerks are common. Some people experience what are called hypnagogic hallucinations during this stage, seeing imaginary objects or people in the room. This is not uncommon in children and usually diminishes with age.

Next we move into stage N2, which is a continuation of stage N1 with the addition of a few extra brain wave events— short bursts of fast brain activity called sleep spindles and K-complexes, which may be important for the integration of new memories with existing knowledge, as well as other aspects of sleep. The brain releases control of our muscles during this stage, as we fall deeper and deeper into sleep.

The next stop is stage N3, sometimes referred to as deep sleep or slow wave sleep. During stage N3, our brain produces very slow, high-amplitude synchronized waves known as delta waves. Delta waves demonstrate that brain circuits are calm and in rhythm. Although the type of dreams that we remember are unlikely to occur during stage N3, terrifying dreams called night terrors can occur during this stage. People who experience night terrors wake up in an emotionally agitated, fearful state, perhaps with no recall of the dream after they wake. Stage N3 is also when sleepwalking and bedwetting are most likely to occur. Because it is associated with these difficulties, N3 sleep is the subject of much investigation these days, but we still don't know very much about how it works or why this stage gives rise to such troubling sleep disturbances.

We do know that the longer we've been awake since our last sleep, and the more mental activity (concentration, thinking, problem solving, dealing with emotions) that occurs right before sleep, the longer we spend in stage N3. This stage appears to be particularly important to the brain. We spend more time in stage N3 earlier in the night than later, suggesting that the brain wants to be certain it gets sufficient stage N3 sleep before moving on.

After stage N3, we go back through stage N2 and then the brain enters rapid eye movement, or REM, sleep. During this stage, brain waves look a lot like the alpha waves that occur during wide-awake thinking, and the sleeping person's eyes dart back and forth behind his closed eyelids. Most dreams that we remember occur during REM, and we find it easiest to wake a person during this stage. Researchers believe that memories from the previous day are stored or consolidated during REM sleep. Interestingly, although both physical and mental exercise during the day lead to an increase in the amount of stage N3 sleep, they actually cause a decrease in REM sleep. As important as REM sleep might be for making memories, the brain appears to want stage N3 sleep more. After REM, we begin the sleep cycle again—stage N2, stage N3, stage N2, REM, repeat. Each cycle lasts approximately ninety minutes.

Setting the Brain's Clock

Several body functions, such as attention, memory, temperature, and hormone levels, roughly follow a twenty-four-hour rhythm known as the circadian rhythm. "Circadian" means "about a day." The brain uses external cues, called zeitgebers (from the German term for "time-givers," or "synchronizers"), to set the internal clock that paces our circadian rhythms. These include things like light, ambient temperature, patterns of social interaction, eating patterns, and even that morning cup of coffee and bedtime reading. Such cues tell the brain where we are in our daily sleep/waking cycle. Without them, the rhythm tends to run longer than twenty-four hours. A disconnection between the cues, as can occur when we travel across time zones, confuses the brain. The disconnection between what time the brain thinks it is and what time the cues say it is leads to jet lag.

Our internal clock is located deep inside the brain in an area of the hypothalamus called the suprachiasmatic nucleus. This little group of brain cells sends out signals to other brain areas indicating what time it is from a biological standpoint. Signals sent to the pineal gland, located near the middle of the brain, trigger the release of melatonin, the hormone that helps us to sleep. Here's how important the suprachiasmatic nucleus is for pacing our sleep and wake cycle: when scientists placed the suprachiasmatic nucleus from a hamster with a twenty-hour daily cycle into a hamster with a twenty-four-hour daily cycle, the latter animal's cycle changed to twenty hours.

The suprachiasmatic nucleus receives signals directly from the eyes. Bright light causes it to signal the pineal gland to stop releasing melatonin. In other words, light tells the pacemaker that it's daytime and we should be awake. That's why early morning sunlight can help a person wake up (and why rock stars often require blackout shades). Similarly, bright light at night can make it harder for a person to fall asleep.

TEEN BRAIN SLEEP CH-CH-CH-CHANGES

Brain activity during sleep changes as we age. The intensity of delta wave activity, associated with stage N3 sleep, decreases by 65 percent between the ages of twelve and seventeen. The intensity of theta wave brain activity, associated with stage N2 sleep, also decreases during adolescence. These changes in sleep waveforms happen during the same general time frame as changes in frontal lobe wiring. Some researchers suggest that the increase in daytime sleepiness that comes with adolescence is partially explained by this reduction in the intensity of delta and theta wave activity when adolescents sleep, though the fact that teens do not get sufficient sleep can't be discounted as a contributing factor.

Daily peak levels of melatonin are also lower in adolescents than in children or adults. And the time of night that melatonin levels reach their peak shifts to a later hour during adolescence. The dip in melatonin levels during adolescence, combined with a peak that comes later in the night, makes it harder for teens to fall asleep at a reasonable hour.

When teens want to stay up late and get up late, they aren't just being lazy or rebellious; they are responding to changing brain activity. However, even with this biological disadvantage, most teens can sleep long enough when the conditions are right. When allowed to sleep as long as they want, teenagers average around nine hours per night. In other words, teenagers are biologically capable of getting enough sleep, they just *don't*. And it's not that they don't want to sleep—indeed, many teens report that they wish they could sleep more. There's just too much homework, socializing, and video games to be taken care of. Not to mention school start times that don't take into account teens' sleeping habits.

How Much Sleep Do Teens Need?

"Once my son entered high school, he started looking and feeling more and more exhausted. He gets the same six to seven hours a night of sleep that I do, but it never seems enough."

Sleep patterns and sleep needs change as we age. The phrase "sleeping like a baby" comes in part from the fact that infants sleep for eighteen hours or more. Experts suggest that teenagers, like children, need about nine hours of sleep per night to perform optimally and maintain good general health. Unfortunately, only one in five teenagers gets this much sleep, and the average number of hours teenagers spend sleeping decreases from 8.3 during eighth grade to 7.3 during twelfth grade. It's even worse in college, where the word "all-nighter" was invented. National surveys reveal a slow and steady decline in the amount of sleep first- and second-year college students get, from roughly 7.75 hours per night in 1969 to 6.65 hours per night in 2001. Sleep patterns are important predictors of overall health and well-being, so it's important to help your teen thrive in this area. For instance:

- Too little sleep during adolescence is associated with a higher likelihood of depression. According to a survey by the National Sleep Foundation, 73 percent of adolescents who report feeling unhappy or depressed also report not getting enough sleep at night and being excessively sleepy during the day.
- Insufficient sleep, particularly on school nights, causes increased levels of the stress hormone cortisol, which alters mood and is toxic to the brain at high enough levels. Sleep-deprived teens show exaggerated stress responses, which interfere with daily activities and well-being.
- Lack of sleep can hurt school performance; students earning A and B grades in high school report greater total sleep time and earlier school night bedtimes than students earning C, D, and F grades.

But, as most adults know, falling asleep can be far from easy, especially if you're feeling stressed or anxious. Research suggests that:

- Kids who ruminate about their problems while in bed or suffer from generalized anxiety are less likely to fall asleep early.
- Among college students, amount of stress has a greater effect on sleep time than caffeine or alcohol use, internet or TV use, or frequency of exercise.
- Problems falling or staying asleep may reflect substance use during adolescence (substance-abusing teens are 3.2 times more likely to experience sleep problems than other teens).

Research has not yet shown whether a certain amount of sleep or a particular pattern of sleep promotes brain development in teens, but it's clear that when teens do hit their optimal nine-hour mark, they're happier and healthier.

SCHOOL STARTS AT *WHAT* TIME?

> *"My daughter has a zero period class that starts at 7 am. That means setting her alarm for 5:45. The earliest she can get to bed with homework, extracurricular activities, dinner, etc., is 11. This is a kid who loves to sleep ten to twelve hours straight. This start time is the worst!"*

Many individuals, including some pediatricians and teenagers, believe that a big part of the problem with teen sleep deprivation relates to how early school starts. School administrators, parents, and doctors across the country have begun using this information to campaign for later start times. In 1996, schools in Edina and Minneapolis delayed school start times at the suggestion of a 1993 report from the Minnesota Medical Association. In Edina, the normal 7:25 am–2:10 pm school day became an 8:30 am–3:10 pm school day, giving teens the opportunity for fifty-five more minutes of sleep. In Minneapolis, the normal 7:15 am–1:45 pm school day became an 8:40 am–3:20 pm school day.

The results were striking. Researchers at the University of Minnesota's Center for Applied Research and Educational Improvement (CAREI) determined that:

- Students slept about an hour more per night
- Attendance improved
- Students were more likely to stay in school
- Students were less tardy
- Students took fewer trips to the school nurse
- Students were more likely to eat breakfast
- There was a calmer school environment with fewer students sent to the principal for disciplinary action
- There were fewer visits to counselors for problems at home or conflicts with peers
- Students displayed extra alertness and efficiency during the day, allowing them to complete more of their homework during school hours

In the years since, several other states, including Kentucky and Massachusetts, have also delayed school start times. As in Minnesota, several important changes were noted in Massachusetts schools, such as increases in sleep time, better school attendance, and higher grades compared to schools in the state that did not change their start time. When schools in

Fayetteville, Kentucky, shifted their start time from 7:30 am to 8:30 am, the number of traffic crashes involving sixteen- to eighteen-year-old drivers decreased.

These findings strongly suggest that teens in school districts with later start times use the extra time to sleep more, and that the extra sleep makes it easier for them to excel in school. Clear scientific findings around school start times are available, and we encourage parents to bring this information to principals and PTAs. This is something you can lobby for! And in the sleep-crusted eyes of your teenager, you may even evolve from useless loser to hero.

The Importance of Bedtime

"My daughter is beyond exhausted when she gets up and during most of the morning and early afternoon. Then she perks up and doesn't even begin to feel tired until midnight. I can't force her to go to bed if she isn't tired, but this kid needs more sleep!"

Since teens are wired to burn the midnight oil, making early mornings rough, some household planning can help. Research suggests that it's possible to get teens on a regular bedtime routine that increases the number of hours they sleep, reduces daytime sleepiness and moodiness, and improves academic performance. One study indicates that adolescents with a bedtime of midnight or later are 24 percent more likely to suffer from depression and 20 percent more likely to think about suicide than teens with a 10 pm bedtime. Parents cannot enforce bedtime on adolescents like they can on young children, and many teens will fight tooth and nail over being treated like a little kid, but talking to your teen about the good biological and cognitive reasons to get adequate sleep can go a long way toward making him or her swallow this bitter pill. Remember, planning is the job of the frontal lobes, which are not fully formed in teens. This is why parents need to help teens plan their evening activities so that they can get to bed at a reasonable hour.

Then, of course, there is the weekend. Sleeping in on weekends is something that most adults dream about and cherish when the opportunity comes along. But what about adolescents? Should parents impose a bedtime routine during the week but allow for maximum sleep on weekends? Some researchers suggest that adolescents go into "sleep debt" during the week due to early school hours, lax bedtimes, and their tendency to stay up late. The term implies that a person can make up for the lost sleep by paying off the debt (i.e. getting more sleep) on weekends. But paying off a sleep debt is not straightforward. Even after prolonged sleep deprivation, the body does not need to make up for each lost hour of sleep. A case in point is Randy Gardner, the *Guinness Book of World Records* holder for going without sleep. In 1964, Randy, a high school student, stayed awake for eleven straight days. After the first four days, he became intermittently delusional and his memory began to fail him. On the eleventh day, he talked to reporters and appeared quite composed. That night, given the chance to sleep as much as he wanted, he slept for just over fourteen hours (a fraction of his sleep debt) and quickly returned to his normal routine. Of course, this does not mean that he had completely erased his sleep debt, just that his general pattern returned to normal pretty quickly. The *Guinness Book of World Records* stopped accepting entries into the sleeplessness category due to concerns about health, so this title will likely always belong to Gardner.

Using the weekend to catch up on missed sleep may be of limited value. The jury is still out on how long it takes to repay a large sleep debt, but our view is that a few hours of extra sleep on the weekend is good if a teen misses getting those important nine hours per night during the week. However, excessive sleeping on the weekend can also throw off sleep rhythms. Research suggests that a big variance between weekday and weekend bedtime routines is associated with adolescent substance use, including cigarettes, marijuana, and alcohol. In girls, a big difference in weekday and weekend sleep patterns was associated with depressed mood. This does not necessarily mean that bedtime variations cause substance abuse or depression—teens with disrupted sleep patterns might be more likely to go out with friends on weekends and to stay out later than others. Statistically, the later teens are out, on weeknights or weekend nights, the more likely they are to encounter alcohol and other drugs.

The bottom line is that big changes in sleep patterns on the weekend may make it tough for teens to readjust to the weekday schedule, adding extra stress and frustration. Healthy sleeping for teens means not only getting enough sleep on any given night, but also having a balanced and consistent sleep-wake pattern across days and weeks.

Tips for Improving Teen Sleep

Sleep is an active brain state that requires action on our part. Establishing healthy sleep routines enhances our lives, keeps our bodies well attuned to their environments, and increases energy and mental clarity. Here are the top ways to improve sleep during the adolescent years (they work for any time of life—so take note!):

- Avoid caffeine after noon. Caffeine stays in the body long enough that a cup of coffee or an energy drink mid-afternoon may interfere with the ability to get to sleep later at night.
- Exercise in the evening, but not too close to bedtime. This can increase the odds of falling asleep and sleeping soundly.
- Maintain a regular pre-bedtime regimen, such as changing into pajamas and brushing your teeth, which signals the brain that bedtime is coming.
- Avoid being in bright light, watching TV, or working on a bright computer screen too close to bedtime. Light tells the brain it's daytime.
- If you can't fall asleep, get out of bed, leave the bedroom and read quietly or engage in some other relaxing activity that doesn't require bright room light. Go back to bed and try again when you feel more tired.
- Avoid the urge to sleep excessively on the weekends, which makes it that much harder to get to sleep on Sunday night and get up on Monday morning. Encourage

Sleeping Pills

Sleep medicines like Lunesta and Ativan are unnecessary for most teens, but can be used in severe cases. Tolerance and dependence are possible with these drugs, so they must be taken under the guidance of a physician. Over-the-counter supplements of the sleep hormone melatonin are another option, but again should only be used under a physician's advisement as melatonin can cause side effects and may interact with other medications.

and arrange activities on weekends that will get teens up within an hour or two of their usual weekday activities.

- Avoid drinking alcohol, which can facilitate getting to sleep but disrupts the late stages of sleep, and as it metabolizes causes hyperactivity in the brain.
- Because anxiety interferes with sleep and sleep restriction triggers more anxiety, it's important to break the cycle through therapy, breathing exercises, physical exercise, and medication. See chapter 2 for more details.

Chapter 5

DRIVING

In *American Graffiti*, an iconic movie about adolescence, teenagers in a small central California town spend their last night before college doing what they've been doing for much of their high school lives: driving. They cruise for chicks, gossip about dudes, and the film climaxes with a drag race between the reigning hot rod champ and the new bad boy in town. Cue exciting music as disaster ensues.

There is a long, rich, and glorious tradition of teens and their love affairs with (and in) cars. While getting a driver's license is a true rite of passage, fantastically liberating for both teen and parent, a car can also be a death trap for teenage drivers, passengers, and innocent travelers alike.

Car crashes claim the lives of more teens than any other cause of death, including murder, suicide, disease, and drug abuse. Roughly one in three teenage deaths result from motor vehicle crashes. According to the Insurance Institute on Highway Safety, 3,115 teenagers (aged thirteen to nineteen) died in car crashes in 2010. An additional 300,000 teens were injured in car crashes but survived. The good news is that these numbers represent significant decreases from previous years; twice as many teenagers died in car crashes in 1975 than 2009. This is probably due to numerous factors, including seatbelt laws, graduated licensing, and rising consciousness of the dangers of drunk driving.

Accounting for poor or risky driving among teens is very complicated. Does neuroscience offer any answers, or provide any guidance for how teens might use their natural abilities while minimizing the liabilities that naturally come with a developing brain? The answer is a resounding yes.

Driving: A Whole Brain Exercise

For adults who drive regularly, driving becomes almost automatic. Gas, brakes, lights, wipers, steering, and stereos are all juggled with relative ease by an experienced driver. You've probably had the experience of driving home from work for the millionth time when you suddenly realize you've made it home without remembering much of the drive. Over time, as driving becomes rote, brain space is freed up to think about other things—like dinner, laundry, and how to become an Internet millionaire. Once driving becomes second nature, it's difficult to appreciate exactly how complicated the task actually is.

As the many small tasks involved in effective driving merge into one continuous flow of activity, a learning process has occurred. But it's not the kind of learning that involves consciously remembering facts. Rather it is memory for movements, sequences of movements, and the coordination of movements. This kind of learning—often referred to as muscle memory—is regulated largely by a primitive part of the brain called the cerebellum, which conducts most of its business below the radar of self-awareness.

The motor cortex and visual cortex are also engaged to get you where you're going safely. The motor cortex, a small vertical strip of tissue under the middle of the skull on both sides of the head, is involved in voluntary, or intentional, movements such as reaching out to grab your cup of coffee or setting out on a walk. Continuing to walk, however, is a well-learned sequence of movements that does not require vigilant attention and can therefore be controlled and monitored by the cerebellum. In driving, the motor cortex is activated when we brake or hit the gas. This is particularly true on the left side of the brain, as the left side controls the right foot, which is typically used for operating the pedals (unless the car also has a clutch, requiring the left foot to participate in the intricate dance of shifting gears).

The occipital lobes, located at the back of the brain where the eyes send information, are also continuously active during driving. Obviously driving requires sustained processing of visual information. Cars and trees whizzing by, traffic signs, depth cues from the car in front, all require the occipital lobes.

Driving is a complex task that requires coordination between all these areas in addition to the sustained attention and quick decision-making enabled by the frontal lobes. A driver must be aware of several variables at once, such as the speed the car is traveling, the position and relative speed of other cars on the road, the conditions of the road (wet, snowy, dry), traffic patterns up ahead, how much gas is in the car, and whether it's time for another cup of coffee. Then, when it comes time to take action, such as shifting lanes or stopping at a traffic light, the frontal lobes must survey the situation and decide how best to proceed by monitoring and influencing the ongoing activity in the other active brain regions. At the same time, the frontal lobes must inhibit unsafe urges, such as running a red light. Obviously, when we drive, the frontal lobes are multitasking in the most critical sense. Because of the way their brains have (and have not) developed—especially when it comes to their frontal lobes—teens face distinct challenges behind the wheel.

Driving on the Wrong Side of the Brain

"How much practice do my twins need before they're ready to drive? Just when I think they're ready, I notice that if there's a new challenge, they're flustered by it and it feels like we're back to square one."

The teen brain is built to learn and to solve problems. Learning how to operate a motor vehicle is pretty easy, and the highly malleable teen brain is fully prepared to learn these basic tasks. But learning to drive and learning to drive *safely* are very different. Safely maneuvering a two-ton vehicle while hurtling through space at speeds in excess of 60 mph requires coordinated activity in several brain areas, in addition to focused attention and strong decision-making skills. Until their brains are able to smoothly handle the complex processing and coordinated activity that enables a driver to execute basic skills and adjust to changing circumstances, driving can be a high-risk activity.

When we first learn to drive, the muscle coordination alone can be challenging—using hands to guide the vehicle while applying appropriate amounts of pressure to gas and brake pedals with the foot. It's like a juggling act. Make it a car with manual transmission and you've added a chainsaw and an egg to the juggling sequence. For a teenager fresh behind the wheel, driving can be a challenging and even nerve-racking experience. The many actions that driving requires eat up precious brain bandwidth and turn it into an ongoing, highly involved task requiring continuous attention. Throw in some rain, a cell phone, or an obnoxious passenger, and demands on the brain increase.

The frontal lobes and the cerebellum are changing during the teen years and do not reach full maturity until the late teens or early twenties. Over years of practice, the multiple tasks of driving get smoothed into easy sequences and become ingrained in the brain as the driver becomes more skilled. But until those skills are established and brain development is largely completed, it is harder for teens to drive than for adults.

Decisions made while driving are also influenced by the social context in which a teen is operating. Around the dinner table, with the threat of grounding and loss of a beloved smart phone, a teenager might sincerely promise to avoid speeding. However, because of his immature frontal lobes, once behind the wheel with friends and music blasting, your teen's driving skills (and common sense) deteriorate and he may speed despite his best intentions.

Why Bad Accidents Happen to Good Teens

"When will I know if my son is safe on the road? He seems nowhere near ready, but I don't know if that's my perception or the reality. Every time he drives, it seems like we narrowly escape death!"

Many teen car accidents can be attributed to simple inexperience behind the wheel. In other cases, inexperience combines with normal adolescent urges to be social, take risks, and show off to contribute to higher accident rates.

Partly due to the undeveloped teenage frontal lobes, when attention is divided between the primary task of driving and other activities, such as talking or changing the radio station, the risk of an accident increases significantly. In driving simulation tasks, teens do just as well as adults when they're alone in the driver's seat. However, when other teens are added to the simulated car, teens take more risks and become more likely than adults to make errors. Adding a single male passenger to a car driven by a sixteen-year-old doubles the risk of being involved in a fatal crash. Speaking of sixteen-year-olds, they are more likely than any other age group (including older teens) to be involved in fatal crashes. The brain circuitry that puts the brakes on risky behaviors and aids in making wise decisions will not be fully developed for another five to ten years.

Heightened risk-taking when friends are in the car helps explain statistics from the Insurance Institute for Highway

Safety. In the real world, the risk of a crash doubles when drivers aged sixteen or seventeen have two friends in the car, and quadruples when three or more friends are present. It's not just that teens' undeveloped brains create an opportunity for distraction: part of the problem is that teens' understanding of the word "risky" differs from that of adults. One recent survey assessed the willingness of drivers to engage in a range of distracting tasks such as dialing cell phones, talking to passengers, eating food, using car navigational systems, and other variables. Teen drivers perceived these tasks to represent less risk for car crashes than adults, and reported more willingness to engage in them while driving.

Due to their still-developing frontal lobes, teens also have difficulty splitting their attention between the requirements of driving and the demands of friends, phones, and music. Teens need all of their mental bandwidth to process the ever-changing information required to drive safely, such as traffic patterns, weather conditions, and stop lights. For young drivers, distractions can be deadly. In one recent study, teens and adults were given driving tasks on a test track. When asked to perform a cell-phone-related task such as dialing a number or answering a phone while approaching an intersection with a traffic light, all of the adults stopped in time. In contrast, one out of four teens failed to stop at the intersection and ran the red light.

According to the Centers for Disease Control and Prevention, teens are also more likely than older drivers to speed and to allow shorter headways (the distance from the front of one vehicle to the front of the next). Roughly 40 percent of male teens and 25 percent of female teens involved in fatal crashes were speeding at the time of the crash. Teens also have the lowest rate of seatbelt use. In 2008, nearly three out of four teen drivers killed in car crashes after drinking and driving were not wearing seatbelts.

The Insurance Institute for Highway Safety has identified other factors that contribute to the likelihood that a teen will be involved in a deadly traffic crash. Nighttime and weekend driving are more hazardous for teen drivers, even when they are compared to drivers just a few years older.

Digital Devices and Driving Don't Mix

There are good studies indicating that the kind of divided attention that cell phone conversations demand degrades one's ability to drive safely. If there are others in the car at the same time, cell phone use can be even more hazardous. And those studies were done on adults. Because teen drivers are already known to be at greater risk for distraction while driving, talking on cell phones creates an opportunity for disaster. And don't even think about texting while driving. Not only is attention dangerously divided, but eyes and hands are focused on punching digits when they should be steering and looking out for danger. Studies have estimated that driving while texting is as dangerous as driving with alcohol intoxication well above the legal limit. Many law enforcement officials now routinely inspect the text transaction records of drivers' cell phones after crashes to determine criminal and civil liability.

Graduated Licensing

"My son was just in an accident where his best friend was driving. There were four kids in the car. I know these kids and I'm convinced the driver was distracted. But my son refuses to tell us what was going on in the car before the accident."

New research on adolescent development combined with statistics showing that sixteen-year-olds are involved in a disproportionate number of car crashes has raised questions about whether sixteen is a reasonable age for kids to drive unsupervised. Most states have moved to tiered or graduated licensing programs that help ease young drivers into the responsibilities and challenges of driving.

Graduated driver licensing (GDL) is a three-tiered approach—learner's permit, restricted license of some sort, followed by full license. New Zealand was the first country to embrace this method, and research indicates that the approach has saved many lives there. It also appears to work in the US. For example, during the first three years after graduated licensing was put in place in North Carolina, fatal traffic crashes involving sixteen-year-old drivers declined by 57 percent. Although not all states show such a marked drop-off in teen traffic crashes, there have been significant decreases across the country now that most states have instituted graduated licensing laws. The most recent studies indicate that the most effective licensing laws incorporate at least five of the following seven provisions:

- A minimum age of sixteen for a learner's permit
- A mandatory waiting period of at least six months before a driver with a learner's permit can apply for a provisional license
- A requirement for 50–100 hours of supervised driving
- A minimum age of seventeen for a provisional license
- Restrictions on driving at night
- A limit on the number of teenage passengers allowed in the car
- A minimum age of eighteen for a full license

One recent study of GDL programs in forty-eight states concluded that the programs reduced traffic fatalities among

The Need for Speed

Many teenagers love to drive fast. Too fast. Once they've reached high speeds, teens are often compelled (more so than adults) to go even faster, take sharp turns, race other drivers, or to try to beat stop lights. Speeding is a common outlet for the adolescent desire to take risks. And without mature frontal lobes, the decision to drive too fast is not just dangerous but life-threatening.

Usually, driving fast or recklessly is a spur-of-the-moment decision—a spontaneous display of machismo or an isolated instance of simple misjudgment. As demonstrated in the famous James Dean drag racing scene in *Rebel Without a Cause*, there's a long tradition of teens driving way too fast for kicks and glory. Extreme driving in movies like *The Fast and the Furious* has glamorized that tendency, turning driving fast into a sport, albeit an illegal and often deadly one, far more organized and far more risky than the spontaneous macho races of decades past. It's difficult to pinpoint exactly how many teens participate in street racing or how many deaths it has caused, because races can be unplanned or mistaken by law enforcement personnel for simple reckless driving.

Street racing brings a momentary rush, but it leads to very serious consequences. Aside from the threat of death or injury, street racers face serious legal consequences; states are beginning to enact tougher laws against this activity, sometimes even fining those who show up just to watch.

Ask your teen if he (this is a trend much more common in boys) is aware of this kind of racing. Explain that this is not a sport but a deadly game. While he may not want to hear your lecture, the warning will register.

drivers aged fifteen to seventeen by 5.6 percent. That might not sound big, but imagine if one of those kids saved by the program is your teenager. That lackluster percentage also appears to be influenced by different levels of effectiveness in implementation of the laws. In states that firmly upheld their GDL requirements, driving fatalities among fifteen- to seventeen-year-olds dropped by 19 percent, while those who did a poor job of implementing their programs saw no decrease in the death rate.

Keeping Teen Drivers Safe

What practical tips can be gleaned from the research on teen brains and driving?

- Have frequent discussions with your teen about the responsibilities and consequences that come with driving. If these ideas are embedded deeply in the memory, they can help teens make better choices once they're behind the wheel.
- Particularly for new drivers, minimize nighttime driving.
- Because distractions like cell phones and friends make it harder for teens to drive safely (particularly for males), house rules should address these issues. Teen drivers should stay off of their phones—and certainly never text—and keep the number of passengers low, preferably at zero.
- Parents should join their teens in promising to minimize these distractions because, even though teens are more susceptible to their dangers, adults are distractible too. And you are the role model for your teen.
- Set up your safe driving expectations before adding your teen to your insurance or paying for a car. And then set up your rules: if you get a speeding ticket, you pay and you lose driving privileges for X number of days, weeks, etc.

Chapter 6

THE DIGITAL WORLD

Al's Diner, the nostalgia-drenched hangout spot in the television show *Happy Days*, was a kind of mythological Shangri-La for American teenagers in the last half of the twentieth century. Boys and girls hung out in packs, eating burgers and fries, and trying to figure out who's going to the prom with whom, while learning what it was to be cool by watching the Fonz intimidate boys and seduce girls. Today, all of that happens (minus the burgers and fries) electronically, with kids jacked into a computer, smart phone, or tablet. In fact, the whole definition of what a "friend" is has changed radically with the advent of electronic communication, which simultaneously makes strangers anonymous and instantly intimate. Today, the Fonz would have a social media page filled with a bevy of beautiful babes, and a tribe of awestruck boys logging in to ogle his life. Al's Diner has morphed into a social network where teenagers are connected not by milkshakes but by text messages, videos, photos, and virtual reality games—for better, and for worse.

The world seems to be moving faster by the second, and teens are getting more and more sophisticated in the ways they interact. So scientists and parents are wondering about how technology affects the development and function of the teenage brain. Parents fear that the mega-hours their teenagers spend reading tens of thousands of text messages, or killing hundreds of thousands of shockingly lifelike humans and/or aliens, will make it hard for them to focus, to socialize and to actually, you know, talk to other human beings.

This Is Your Brain on Social Media

In the digital age, gathering information involves scanning and skimming. Today's adolescents dart like water bugs between Google searches, Facebook updates, goofy videos of milk spewing out of noses, all the while furiously typing life-and-death text messages. In real time. This requires the brain to rapidly shift attention and engage in lots of information processing strategies—deciphering text message language, the meaning of images, and verbal conversations—simultaneously or in quick succession. This is a very different way of learning from quietly reading the Sunday paper, taking an occasional phone call on a land line, or sitting around a campfire telling stories. As Nicholas Carr argues in his book *The Shallows*, "What we're experiencing is, in a metaphorical sense, a reversal of the early trajectory of civilization: we are evolving from being cultivators of personal knowledge to being hunters and gatherers in the electronic data forest."

In order to meet these new demands, the brain reorganizes itself. Learning to process information streaming through digital media requires the development of brand new cognitive abilities in still-developing teenage brains. Patricia Greenfield, a psychologist at the University of California, argues in a 2009 issue of *Science*:

> Every medium has its strengths and weaknesses; every medium develops some cognitive skills at the expense of others. Although the visual capabilities of television, video games, and the Internet may develop impressive visual intelligence, the cost seems to be deep processing: mindful knowledge acquisition, inductive analysis, critical thinking, imagination, and reflection ... Yet society needs reflection, analysis, critical thinking, mindfulness, and imagination more than ever. The developing human mind still needs a balanced media diet, one that is not only virtual, but also allows ample time for the reading and auditory media experiences that lead to these important qualities of mind.

The brain functions and develops differently according to the demands placed on it to process information, and to the type of information received. In the electronic age, information is received rapid-fire, in many forms, and seems to demand an immediate response. The brain can certainly adapt to what many parents see as a bombardment of information, but when that happens during the teen years, while the brain is sculpting itself into adulthood, what are the long-term implications for brain function? It may surprise you to learn that recent studies reveal as many positive effects as negative ones. And while there is still much to discover, we know that the teen brain is built to take in massive amounts of information with unprecedented speed, and to adapt accordingly.

Social Animals and Cyber Peeps

"I really got to know my friends. We talked on the phone every night, had sleepovers every weekend, spent dinners with each other's families. How can Facebook possibly provide this kind of deep friendship?"

When teenagers hang out online instead of in person, does this somehow make their friendships and social relationships more superficial? Does it retard the ability to interact successfully in person? The early answer seems to be no. This digital world is not turning our teens into socially isolated automatons who can't interact face to face. In fact, the evidence thus far suggests the opposite. Online socializing can have positive effects on friendships, and it provides socially anxious teens with a valuable tool through which they can take a slow and safe approach to building friendships. With research by the Pew Center suggesting that 95 percent of US teens use the Internet and that 80 percent of those use social networking sites, this is good news indeed.

The circuits exercised in the brains of teenagers texting, e-mailing, and hanging out online are not the circuits exercised during face-to-face contact. There are many brain processes at work, beyond merely interpreting language and speech, when it comes to face-to-face communication. Odors powerfully influence emotional activity in the amygdala and alter how both verbal and nonverbal information is processed and interpreted by the brain. Body language, posture, and eye movement tell us when the words someone is speaking are out of sync with what they actually think and feel. These cues help us read between the lines. While text messages and posts on social media communicate meaning, the meaning must be derived from words alone, since facial expressions, body language, and other subtle, sometimes intuitive, communications are stripped out. As texts, tweets, and instant messages have become more and more popular, we must deal with the absence of those nonverbal nuances more frequently. And, though emoticons offer substitutes for facial expressions, they're obviously not the same. The impact of all that stripped-down communication is now the subject of considerable study by psychologists, neuroscientists, and communications specialists.

Digital communication relies largely on the written word. The interpretation of written words is mostly provided by a region of the neocortex called Wernicke's area, located at the intersection between the temporal and parietal lobes on the side of the cortex. Karl Wernicke, the German physician who first characterized the function of this brain area in 1876, noticed that people who have damage in this region lose the ability to understand language. Wernicke's area connects to a region in the frontal lobe called Broca's area, identified by the French neurosurgeon Paul Broca in 1861. While Wernicke's area is needed to understand language, Broca's area is needed to produce language. So, if Wernicke's area is damaged but Broca's area is not, a person can write and speak but can't understand what they are reading or what someone is saying. If someone has damage to Broca's area but not to Wernicke's area, they cannot communicate with words but can still understand what they read and hear. Before this relationship was understood, many patients with damage to Broca's area were thought to be completely unaware of what was happening around them. In fact, they knew exactly what was happening, they just couldn't tell anyone.

In the vast majority of people, both Wernicke's area and Broca's area are located on the left side of the brain. But the left and right sides of our brains communicate so extensively with each other, it is generally inaccurate to ascribe functions to just one side. Language is probably as close as a function gets to a one-sided activity, but even it requires both sides. Jokes, for instance, are far more than just collections of words. And sentences like "I ran into my friend at the mall" require a larger context in order to be understood. An awareness of the emotions conveyed by words and the ways in which the words are spoken or written requires brain processing beyond Wernicke's and Broca's areas. The emotional, big-picture interpretations are performed in the right side of the brain, making language a whole-brain exercise after all.

When reading a text, for example, the emotional areas in the brain are activated after the circuits in Wernicke's area interpret the meaning of the words. The brain uses its interpretation to determine the appropriate emotional reaction. But during "live" social interactions, there are many cues that directly activate the emotional areas of the brain. The amygdala, the reward system, and the hypothalamus are all simultaneously engaged as words are interpreted. A smile or a subtle raise of an eyebrow, a sigh, a touch on the arm, the smell of perfume, the lighting in the room, and many other cues lead to a richer, more immediate, and more layered interaction.

2 txt r nt 2 txt

Does your teen send a gazillion text messages every day? Or does it just seem that way? One-third of teen texters send more than one hundred texts per day. A study conducted by the Pew Research Center indicates that cell phones have become the primary means of communication for today's adolescents. Roughly 75 percent of twelve- to seventeen-year-olds own cells phones, up from 45 percent in 2004. The majority of US teens (72 percent) use text messages to communicate, and more than half of teens (54 percent) text daily. For a whole generation of teenagers, texting has become the norm for casual communication. According to the Pew Research Center, 59 percent of girls and 42 percent of boys text friends several times a day "just to say hello." Indeed, text messaging outranks talking face to face with friends (only 33 percent of teens do this in a typical day), e-mailing friends (11 percent), or even having conversations with friends on cell phones (38 percent). Naturally, texting has filtered into the classroom, causing many schools to limit the use of cell phones, to restrict calls to emergencies, or to ban them altogether. Still, 40 percent of teens text in class, 17 percent of in-class texters report that they do it "constantly," and 22 percent report that they have texted answers to classmates who were struggling to answer a teacher's question. Of course, for generations, students have passed notes, created elaborate codes, and devised ingenious ways to communicate without being detected. But texting creates a near-instantaneous and easy-to-hide option that already has its own ever-flexible language. Cyber cheating is just the latest in a long and glorious tradition of kids trying to pull a fast one on the grownups. But let's not be so quick to put the blame for excessive text messaging on our teenagers . . . two-thirds of them reported that their parents texted them during the school day!

Just because digital processing is less complex doesn't mean it is without value. Whether Facebook is used to communicate, as a virtual diary, or just to explore what "friends" and friends alike are doing, the process seems to be rewarding. Social scientists at Cornell University found that having college students view and update their personal profiles on Facebook boosted their self-esteem, and other studies have shown that, just like actual socializing, using sites like Facebook helps people relax. Researchers at the University of Missouri had college students spend five minutes on Facebook while measuring electrical conductance across their skin—a physiological measure of how nervous or anxious a person is. They found that social searching—looking at a friend's profile information, looking through the friend's pictures, and reading messages—was associated with a decrease in skin conductance. Just perusing someone's personal information or adding photos, videos, links, or little bits of their lives to their Facebook page can be relaxing to teenagers and boost feelings of well-being and self-esteem. So while Facebook offers lots of ways to interact and communicate directly with others, it may also be used in a more solitary way, like a digital equivalent of worry beads or petting a dog.

It feels good to fly solo in the cyber world, observing the universe from the safety of your own little digital corner. But, it turns out, it also feels good to play with others on the information superhighway. A 2010 study from the department of psychology at Brock University in Canada looked at how digital socializing (communicating and hanging out with friends online) affects the quality of friendships. Rather than taking a snapshot of relationship quality in time, the researchers followed teen subjects from ninth grade through the end of high school. They found that girls who regularly engaged in online socializing reported more positive friendship quality during the high school years than did their peers who rarely engaged in online socializing. For boys it was different—online socializing did not change the quality of friendships during the high school years.

Interestingly, when the scientists at Brock looked at teens with social anxiety disorder, they found that online socializing was associated with a *better* quality of friendships in both boys and girls. Hanging out with friends online might actually turn out to be useful in helping teens connect with people in a meaningful way. The buffer of the online connection frees socially anxious teenagers to express themselves more intimately and thus begin to overcome inhibiting worries about how they're perceived.

The Canadian study also debunks a common misconception among parents: that being on a sports team, for example, will help your teen make and maintain meaningful friendships but Facebooking with a "friend" all day will not. When the Canadian study looked at the effect of participation in organized sports on friendship quality, here's what they found: nada. Sports participation did not affect friendship quality regardless of whether teens were socially anxious or not. That may seem counterintuitive, but strong friendships in teenagers often involve the direct sharing of personal information, which is frequently discouraged among teenagers in organized sports. The anonymity of digital information makes it much easier for this sharing to happen online. Studies show that when young people interact digitally, they disclose more personal information than when they interact face to face. We all know the risks of revealing personal information online, whether by congressmen or teenagers, but there is also a positive side to the coin. Doctors report that it's like pulling teeth to get certain kinds of health-related information from teens, but they are more likely to reveal risky sexual practices and drug use when filling out surveys on a computer in a doctor's office than when filling them out on paper or talking to the doctor directly. Thus, with the help of digital devices, doctors can obtain crucial information that helps in diagnosing and treating teenagers.

Internet counseling has been shown to ease symptoms of depression and anxiety as well. Because of their familiarity with and trust in digital media, young people may simply feel more freedom to reveal themselves and share personal information by writing words and pushing a button than by having to talk about intimate matters while looking into someone's eyes. A dozen studies of Internet-based mental health programs in Australia concluded that an online computerized cognitive behavioral therapy program called MoodGYM eases symptoms of anxiety and depression in school-aged children.

Other research shows that adolescents, including those with social anxiety, felt that there were times when online socializing made it easier for them to be their "real selves." Online friendships seem to create a comfortable environment for socially anxious adolescents to interact more intimately with their peers, in ways that they can't with more traditional adolescent activities.

The Upside of 'Screen Time'

While Internet use seems to go hand in hand with higher friendship quality among teens, it also seems to breed weaker parental relationships. More Internet time leaves less time for Mom and Dad. This can be an annoyance to parents, resulting in angry sighs and exacerbated proclamations: "Turn off the computer, all you do is sit in front of that thing all day!" This is typically followed by the rolling of teenage eyes and disgruntled muttering. But remember that teens are separating from the family and finding greater importance in peer relationships. Breaking away from parents is a natural part of the developmental process, and Internet use seems to facilitate a natural transition toward independence and self-reliance.

While many parents bemoan the proliferation of social media, we can all rest a little easier knowing that our teens are able to thrive via digital communication—and maybe even teach their parents how to adapt to these new tools as well.

Lost and Found in the Land of Games

"I wasn't so much concerned about what my teenager was doing while he was on the computer. It was more about what things he wasn't doing. Being outside, playing sports, hanging out with his friends, having real-life adventures instead of cyber ones."

More and more teens are finding their niches and forming meaningful relationships through multiplayer games in which warriors, wizards, and warlocks team up with kings, ninjas, and princesses all over the galaxy. They are not necessarily playing with friends they already know; 27 percent of teens play these games with people they meet online. Online gaming often keep teens (and many adults) at the computer for hours, and has contributed to many a "lost weekend."

The very plastic adolescent brain learns about the world by using positive and negative feedback to shape behavior. If a strategy satisfies a need, then that strategy becomes etched into the brain as a habit. If the strategy doesn't work, the impulse wanes. So, adolescents who are consistently rejected or unappreciated by their peers may lose interest in having successful, happy relationships. Traditionally, teenagers who were anxious, clumsy, nervous, or otherwise awkward were at a severe disadvantage, because they were forced to interact face to face, and their lack of social skills inhibited them from forming meaningful connections with neighbors, classmates, and teammates alike. They were wallflowers, loners, outsiders. Some persevered and became president of the chess club, comic book artists, or science geeks who studied brains. But online games offer a new solution. In a game such as World of Warcraft, the teen who can't make eye contact can gain a reputation as a mighty warrior. In a game like Second Life, a person with limited social skills can become a successful businessperson or a swinging playboy. The virtual world can be very compelling—particularly for someone who has had little social success in the real one. Though gaming may seem to a parent like a solitary activity, it often involves rich, complex, and meaningful contact with other real people.

Playing computer games has also been shown to enhance spatial and reading skills. On the other hand, playing violent video games has been related to increased aggressiveness (see chapter 9). Parents should take a balanced view of the hours spent gaming; while limiting or banning exposure to video game violence makes a lot of sense, limiting or banning time spent comfortably socializing via gaming does not.

The Terrible Power of Viral Humiliation

"My daughter posted a photo of herself on Facebook. When she returned to her post a few hours later, several mean girls

in her class wrote how fat she looked. Then they started
sharing the photo with all of their 'friends,' with even more
cutting comments attached. This has been one of the most
challenging and horrifying experiences I've gone through
as a parent. And I've been through a lot."

While the opportunities for digital socializing have grown
exponentially since the dawn of the technological era, so
have the pitfalls. In the past, bullies who pushed other kids
around on the playground were easy to identify. These days,
bullies use the Internet to launch their attacks under the
cloak of e-anonymity. And in a world where almost everyone
has a smart phone which records audio and video, teens post
and circulate records of their lives with unprecedented ease
and frequency on the Internet—which can carry devastating
social and personal costs. Adolescents are known for being
impulsive, and what in the past might have been a quickly
forgotten youthful prank, or a small lapse in judgment, is
now recorded and watched over and over again by friends,
enemies, relatives, employers, college admissions officers, and
total strangers.

Though it inflicts some of the same deep psychological
wounds as real-life bullying, the world of cyber bullying is a
shadowy one. Parents are well schooled in the long and igno-
minious tradition of playground bullying and the cult of the
mean girl, but many parents are not even aware that such a
world exists online or that it affects their kids. In one recent
study, only 15 percent of parents were aware that cyber bullying occurs, while 42 percent of kids reported having been

bullied online and 35 percent reported receiving some form of direct threat against them. Half of all middle school students in one study had visited websites created by bullies to torment classmates.

The Internet creates a perfect storm for cyber bullying. Malicious kids—and some malicious adults—can torment others easily, cheaply, and daily without putting themselves at immediate risk of getting caught. A kid who might not have enough moxie, motivation, or physical prowess to bully others face to face may find the cyber world a much safer place to inflict misery on others. Being anonymous also emboldens bullies to be even crueler than they might be in face-to-face encounters. The National Crime Prevention Council describes some of the ways in which teens bully one another online. A bully may spread lies and rumors, or impersonate someone else and do the same thing, leading classmates to believe that that person is spreading rumors, threatening others, etc. Composing or forwarding mean text messages, and posting real and/or digitally altered pictures of people without their consent, are other ways in which cyber bullies get at their victims. Of course, this humiliation is no longer limited by physical proximity. It can travel all over the world in the blink of an eye.

Cyber bullying can be even more damaging than face-to-face bullying. When a bullied kid can identify the source of aggression and insensitivity, there is hope that the bully can be reined in by parents, teachers, or even legal intervention. It is not that easy on the Internet, where bullies can hide or impersonate others.

Cyber bullying places enormous stress on victims, and as detailed in chapter 2, teens handle stress differently from adults. Since adolescents are so motivated by social reward, they are also very averse to its withdrawal. In the cyber world, someone can post a nasty comment on a Facebook page, Twitter account, or YouTube for all of the victim's friends, family, teammates, teachers, coaches, college admissions officers, etc., to see, making a teen feel like the whole world is against her. Without the perspective and control that comes with fully developed frontal lobes, bullied teens may feel that they don't have any options other than self-destructive behavior. While adults are able to look at a problem in the present, see where it might lead, and come up with a well-reasoned, sensible, and effective series of actions to reverse it and move forward, teens have less capacity for calm planning and self-regulation. Without a clear sense of the future, they may feel that their only choice is a quick, strong, impulsive reaction. Some teens feel, after one bad day, that their life is over, as can be seen in a number of recent high-profile cases where teens committed suicide after cyber bullying incidents.

To help a teen contend with bullying, everyone from parents, teachers, siblings, and friends must understand that the teen's feelings of hopelessness are real and overpowering. Adults can also help bullied teens to recognize that there will be a time in the future when the emotional agony ends. Helping a teen to envision a future that they are unable to see for themselves can be a salve to teens who are unable to self-soothe.

I Heart You

"If a Congressman named Wiener can't stop himself from posting a picture of his most private body part over Twitter, how am I to expect my teenager not to get hot and heavy on the Internet?"

There are a number of online dating services for teens and, if the current trend among adults is any indication, a sizeable percentage of teens will go on to form romantic relationships in the virtual world before meeting in the real one. Indeed, the online dating service eHarmony boasts that it is responsible for 2 percent of US marriages, which equals more than 40,000 marriages a year. The challenge for teens is to handle romantic relationships formed online or maintained via online communication with common sense and an eye to the future. Neither of these is easy for teens.

Whether the emotion is fear, anger, or love, the adolescent brain is primed to develop strong reactions to other people. This is partly because, as we've discussed, the adolescent brain is highly responsive to reward, and the reward system is fueled by feelings of attraction. From a biological standpoint, this helps to ensure that young people form sexual relationships and reproduce. The reward system in the adolescent brain is different from the adult's in important ways. Specifically, it drives behavior more powerfully in adolescents because they are more responsive to reward (pleasure), including social reward, than adults. The brain's reward system is not the only actor in this play. The frontal lobes, which are so critical for judgment, planning, and decision-making, are struggling to catch up with rapidly maturing brain regions that promote sexual attraction and the urge to reproduce. Teens have the bodies and the brain functions to be reproductive adults, and the overpowering impulses to act on these feelings. It is up to their immature frontal lobes to keep the train on the tracks, and unfortunately this doesn't always happen. So, when an adolescent gets a bit of titillating romantic reinforcement, he will be more responsive to it than an adult. And with access to instant digital communication, a teen has the potential both to be much more intimate than his precursors could have been, and to be more easily hurt.

One difficulty of romantic digital communication is that the nonverbal elements are missing. As a result, words can easily be misinterpreted. Because of teenagers' underdeveloped frontal lobes, their minds are more likely to run wild with the possibilities of digital romantic communication. Messages that might be interpreted by adults cautiously may be met by teens with more impulsive, emotional, irrational, and reward-driven thoughts like, "Wow, she likes me! I've got to get over to her house right now!"

Parents should make the risks of digital romance very clear to teens, lest their words and images come back to haunt them, especially when it comes to "sexting"— the act of sending sexually explicit messages via text. Most teenagers who sext see it as a way to be intimate with their girlfriend or boyfriend and are unaware of the risks involved. Of course there are plenty of risks involved in face-to-face sexual behavior, but once a digital message or a naked picture is sent or posted it has the potential to go anywhere there is a computer and to be stored permanently. A rash of ex-girlfriend and ex-boyfriend porn sites have popped up all over the Internet, and a sexually explicit PowerPoint presentation created by a college student recently went viral and made national news. Several recent teen suicides have been linked to such scenarios.

One way to help prevent potentially destructive and dangerous sexual behavior in this digital age is to pay for your teen's cell phone. Teens whose parents pay are less likely than teens who pay for their own cell phone plans to send nude or nearly nude pictures or videos of themselves.

The Pornographication of the Teenage Brain

"I caught my son looking at porn on his computer. I also looked at porn at his age. But what I looked at is nothing compared to what's available online today. I wanted to have an honest conversation with him, but I didn't know where to start. It was one of those awkward parenting moments where you just want to pretend nothing happened. And stupidly, that's what I did."

1969: "Let's see, what can I hide it under? Two packs of gum, a Coke, a pack of baseball cards, one copy of *Sports Illustrated*. Okay, be cool, the clerk isn't looking . . . one copy of *Playboy* tucked underneath. Maybe he'll just ring it all up and not say anything. I sure hope that lady over there doesn't get in line behind me."

Today: Click.

Some of us remember when acquiring pornography

involved a substantial risk of embarrassment, and storing it required finding a place that your parents would never discover. These days an endless stream of digital pornography is just a click away and is easily erased or stored on tiny flash drives or digital devices that parents may not even know how to work.

Porn has long been, if not the backbone, then certainly the heated groin of the Internet since it first came into popular use. By 2006 there were at least 420 million pornography websites, and the pornography industry generated $97 billion in revenue—more than Microsoft, Google, Amazon, eBay, Yahoo, Apple, and Netflix combined. But many pornography sites are free and are very easily accessed by anyone with an Internet connection. In surveys, anywhere between 21 and 71 percent of adolescents report being exposed to online pornography. For boys, the numbers are higher. But despite the high percentage of teens who access online pornography, 46 percent of females and 23 percent of males describe it as "degrading." This ambivalence may reflect the conflict between natural adolescent curiosity and drive toward sexually charged stimuli and the very explicit nature of the sexual images available online; the intensity of the images may be more than they bargained for. In addition, one study showed that 25 percent of US teens had come into unwanted contact with pornography through digital media; of those, 73 percent had encountered it while surfing the Internet and 27 percent encountered it after opening an e-mail or clicking on a link within an e-mail or instant message. Still, there is plenty of intentional pursuit of pornography among US teens; 25 percent of males and 5 percent of females report intentionally viewing sexually explicit material online. Many teens view such material at least once a week. Among eighteen- to twenty-one-year-olds, 87 percent of men view pornography—50 percent weekly and 20 percent daily or every other day—and 31 percent of college-age women view pornography as well.

Will exposure to Internet pornography alter the trajectory of teens' sexual development for the worse—or for the better? Recent studies support the concern that teens' views about sex can be altered by pornography, resulting in more permissive attitudes, but exposure to pornography does not seem to promote the development of a purely recreational attitude toward sex, which may impair a teen's ability to build substantive relationships. For more on pornography, see Chapter 7.

Computing Time on the Computer

"I am confused by how to regulate my teen's time on the computer. She is required by her teachers to do a lot of work on the computer. And she is very social, so she spends a ton of time on Facebook and such. She also shops online, posts videos on YouTube, and who knows what else. What is an okay amount of computer time? Help!"

Many parents embrace the use of gathering information via the Internet but remain concerned about the impact of Internet use on academic success and social relationships. In one recent study, researchers found that computer use generally decreased during the high school years for girls, but not for boys. The main difference was that boys tended to continue playing computer-based video games through the high school years, whereas girls tended to give them up along the way.

This study also revealed an interesting relationship between Internet use and academic performance and attitude. A measure of "academic orientation" was used to capture not only the students' grades but also their educational aspirations, how likely they were to plan ahead academically, how likely they were to feel bored at school, and how important it was for them to do well in school. There was a strong relationship between Internet use and academic orientation, but it wasn't simply that more or less was better. The students with the most positive academic orientation scores were those who used the Internet approximately three to four hours per day, so we can conclude that Internet use actually caused the posi-

---

I Can't Hear You, I'm Plugged In

Cell phones are not the only devices commonly seen affixed to the heads of teens. Earbuds or headphones attached to digital music players have become increasingly common. Hearing loss among adolescents is up 30 percent over the last few decades, and many scientists and physicians suspect this jump may be the result of long hours of listening to loud music through headphones. Indeed, today's teens spend roughly twice as much time listening to music using headphones than teens in previous decades. If the vibrations affecting the eardrums and other structures are too strong and the ear is exposed for too long, it is possible to damage the tiny sound receptors and inhibit the ability to hear. The risks appear to be higher when using earbud headphones, which stick into rather than cover the ear, and even higher with the type of earbud that is molded to fit into the auditory canal and allow no airspace between the sound generator and the canal. This means that the sound is not even dampened a little bit by having to travel across some air space before heading into the auditory canal, and the risk of dangerously high volume levels is increased. Of course, all of this risk is mitigated if the user simply keeps the volume down.

For teens, the risks associated with exposure to loud sounds may be greater than for adults. One recent study from the University of Haifa showed differences in auditory information processing between people fourteen and eighteen years old. This suggests that the development of hearing continues through adolescence, contrary to the long-held view that the auditory system has finished developing by about the age of ten. Another recent study from McGill University suggests that the auditory cortex may still be changing in the way it processes sounds through adolescence and into early adulthood. As we've noted in other chapters, the developing circuits of the teenage brain are changing rapidly; a developing auditory cortex may be more vulnerable to damage or rearrangement. Although we'll have to wait for more specific research to know for sure, the existing information certainly suggests that teens' exposure to loud and sustained sounds should be limited.

tive orientation. Less than that or more than that, and the academic orientation scores were significantly worse.

Now that we know that a certain amount of online time is associated with good academic and social outcomes, parents can use this data to take an objective look at the amount of time their kids spend online. Being able to present this concrete information to your teen may help avoid an emotional discussion in which you're labeled "hopelessly out of touch."

Chapter 7

SEX AND SEXUALITY

If you want to make teenagers cringe, blush and shudder, ask them about their parents having sex. Now ask parents about their kids having sex. Same goes. But the fact is that our kids' brains program them to become sexual beings, whether we like it or not.

In adolescence, the brain prepares us psychologically, socially, emotionally, and neurologically for how to mate and procreate. But few teens are consciously thinking about having babies and raising children—and many are in outright denial of the consequences of exchanging bodily fluids. But they are dreaming and scheming about how to hook up and have sex . . . *a lot*. Sex is on the adolescent brain. For teen boys in particular, it can dominate.

We used to think of puberty and adolescence as driven by a runaway train called hormones. If we were writing this a decade ago, puberty might have been the central focus of the entire book. We might have discussed how we can't blame our kids for acting crazy because their hormone levels are out of control. That idea lives on in mainstream culture, and hormone changes do contribute to adolescent behavior. But surging hormone levels can't account for every teenage action. While puberty and adolescence overlap, they're not the same. Puberty—which stems from the Latin word *pubes*, hair— refers to hormone changes that result in a physical growth spurt, and development of primary sex characteristics (sperm, menstruation) and secondary ones (pubic hair, changes in distribution of muscle and fat, facial hair). Puberty is the physical preparation that allows a developing person to mate and procreate. But these changes don't just happen below the neck. We now know that changes in the adolescent brain have a profound influence on sexual behavior, and play a part in determining whether your teenager will grow up to have a sex life that's joyful, self-destructive, or bumping along the road somewhere in between. These changes are occurring hand in hand with all the other brain changes we've discussed, making teens' sex lives tough terrain to navigate.

To date, there is very little research on teen sexuality that is based directly on brain science. But there's one thing we know for sure: we can't expect teens to turn their sexuality off. Biology won't let them. Try as you might, there's nothing you can do to stop this natural process from unfolding.

The Battle of the Teenage Sexes

Before we tackle teen sexuality, let's take a moment to talk about the difference in brains between the sexes. Girls enter puberty earlier than boys and their brains seem to start undergoing adolescent changes earlier, too. Peak brain size is reached at about eleven years of age in girls and fifteen years of age in boys. While male brains are about 10 percent larger than female brains, perhaps due to a greater number of neurons, this has no effect on intelligence. In fact, girls tend to do better than boys in the following areas during their adolescent years (and perhaps into adulthood as well):

- Girls tend to be better at reading people's emotions and being empathetic. This may relate to anatomical differences between boys and girls in a part of the prefrontal cortex called the straight gyrus.
- Girls form stronger social bonds with peers than boys do, probably because they tend to be better at perceiving and interpreting social cues. Again, this skill is correlated with the differing anatomy of the straight gyrus.
- Girls have a larger corpus callosum—the bundle of neurons connecting the two sides of the brain—which may allow them to organize thoughts and emotions more quickly than boys.
- Girls have better reading and writing skills and larger vocabularies than boys, as well as larger language-related brain regions such as Broca's area.

Don't despair if you have sons! They've got stuff going for them that girls don't:

- Boys have stronger math skills than girls during adolescence, but not childhood.
- Boys are better than girls at mentally picturing and rotating 3-D objects.

Of course, adolescents are not statistics, and their skills vary greatly both within the sexes and between them. Some boys are much stronger in the language arts than in mathematics, while some girls have stellar math skills compared to their brothers.

Girls do have one big advantage over boys in terms of brain development. It appears that they have more white matter connections (the "wires" that transfer messages between different brain regions) in place earlier in adolescence than boys, which allows the various parts of the female brain to work together more smoothly earlier on. This would explain why girls master things like planning and the integration of emotions at a young age. Boys show a steeper rate of increase in white matter during later adolescence (up to about age twenty-four), which may account for the long-standing observation that teen girls seem more mature than teen boys.

The Real Story on Hormones

During the first ten years of life, the external differences between males and females can be subtle. By the time puberty ends, girls will look like women and boys like men. Cascading changes in hormone levels are at the heart of these physical changes, and likely kick off the other brain changes that occur during adolescence.

Hormones are chemical messengers that affect cells in the body by plugging into special receptors on those cells. They are released into the bloodstream by glands and taken everywhere that blood goes. Any cell in the body that has special receptors for a particular hormone will respond to it once it arrives, no matter how far away it is from the gland that released the hormone. In this way, glands use hormones to shout messages to any cell that has the receptors to listen. The end result is that hormones released from a small gland can evoke widespread changes in how the body looks and functions.

The changes that happen during puberty begin deep inside the brain. The hypothalamus triggers the pituitary gland to release hormones. If you point one finger at your temple and another right between your eyes, the lines would intersect at your pituitary gland (the word pituitary, as sophisticated as it sounds, means snot, because that's what early neuroanatomists thought the gland made). Hormones released by the hypothalamus and pituitary gland travel through the blood to endocrine glands (special tissues that create and release their own hormones) located throughout the body. Such glands include the testes in males and the ovaries in females, the thyroid gland that controls metabolism, and the adrenal glands that release adrenaline and cortisol in times of stress. The hypothalamus monitors the blood to check levels of hormones in the body, signaling the endocrine glands to increase or decrease hormone release to keep things at the desired level. So, the hypothalamus works like a thermostat; when hormone levels are too high, the hypothalamus stops telling the pituitary to signal the endocrine glands to release hormones. If levels are too low, the hypothalamus tells the pituitary to send signals to release more hormones.

At the onset of puberty, the hypothalamus and pituitary change the signals they send to distant glands, which causes the body to begin transforming itself from child to adult. Between the ages of eight and ten—usually closer to eight for girls and ten for boys—the hypothalamus starts to release a hormone called gonadotropin releasing hormone (GnRH). GnRH travels the short distance to the pituitary and triggers the release of two other hormones: follicular stimulating hormone (FSH) and leuteinizing hormone (LH). These two hormones enter the bloodstream and eventually reach the testes in boys and the ovaries in girls, causing the testes to release testosterone, an androgen, and the ovaries to release estradiol, an estrogen. A common misconception is that only men have testosterone and only women have estradiol (usually just called estrogen). In fact, males and females use both estradiol and testosterone during development, but males use more testosterone, and females more estrogen. Once the hypothalamus kicks things off, puberty begins, and it's off to the races.

I Don't Like That Attitude!

Just as they contain receptors for neurotransmitters, many neurons also contain receptors for hormones, which means that along with initiating physical changes, hormones will affect the brain, and therefore thinking and mood, as well. As the menstrual cycle cranks up and gets going full steam, levels of hormones rise and fall and the female brain is bathed in varying levels of these powerful molecules. So females often experience a dip in mood in the week leading up to menstruation as both estrogen and progesterone levels decline. An estimated nine out of ten girls reported bad moods just prior to menstruation. Research suggests that girls tend to feel best in the middle of a cycle and that anxiety and depression tend to creep in as the cycle comes to a close. On the flip side, girls do better on tests of memory, concentration, motor coordination, and reaction time during the third week of their cycle. In short, the monthly cascade of hormonal changes does more than prepare the body for pregnancy; it also influences how women think, feel, and act.

While there is no equivalent to menstruation in boys, higher testosterone levels do change boys' behavior at the onset of puberty, increasing confidence levels, sexual urges, and competitive play. But we don't know nearly as much about how testosterone modulates brain activity as we do about estrogen.

Either way, it's important for teenagers to understand why their bodies, including their brains, feel like roller coasters. If parents can make teens aware of the hormonal changes affecting their moods, they may more easily see the light at the end of the tunnel during their darker moments.

The Word of the Day Is: Sex

"I want my son to know that sex is not an extracurricular activity—that it has meaning and should occur in the context of a relationship. But kids today seem so much more interested in hooking up once and that's it."

Generation after generation, adults think that every new wave of adolescents is exercising worse judgment than they

Percentage of Americans Performing Certain Sexual Behaviors in the Past Year (N=5865)

SEXUAL BEHAVIORS	AGE GROUPS									
	14-15		16-17		18-19		20-24		25-29	
	Men	Women	Men	Women	Men	Women	Men	Women	Men	Women
Masturbated Alone	62%	40%	75%	45%	81%	60%	83%	64%	84%	72%
Masturbated with Partner	5%	8%	16%	19%	42%	36%	44%	36%	49%	48%
Received Oral from Women	12%	1%	31%	5%	54%	4%	63%	9%	77%	3%
Received Oral from Men	1%	10%	3%	24%	6%	58%	6%	70%	5%	72%
Gave Oral to Women	8%	2%	18%	7%	51%	2%	55%	9%	74%	3%
Gave Oral to Men	1%	12%	2%	22%	4%	59%	7%	74%	5%	76%
Vaginal Intercourse	9%	11%	30%	30%	53%	62%	63%	80%	86%	87%
Received Penis in Anus	1%	4%	1%	5%	4%	18%	5%	23%	4%	21%
Inserted Penis into Anus	3%		6%		6%		11%		27%	

did. When it comes to sex, today's teens are actually making better choices than their parents. While it's true that teenagers are having lots of sex, they are having less of it than teens of a few decades ago.

Given that for millennia humans lived to be an average of only twenty-something years old, it's understandable that our sexuality blossomed early. Now, the ability—or rather, biologi-

SEXUAL BEHAVIORS	AGE GROUPS									
	30–39		40–49		50–59		60–69		70+	
	Men	Women	Men	Women	Men	Women	Men	Women	Men	Women
Masturbated Alone	80%	63%	76%	65%	72%	54%	61%	47%	46%	33%
Masturbated with Partner	45%	43%	38%	35%	28%	18%	17%	13%	13%	5%
Received Oral from Women	78%	5%	62%	2%	49%	1%	38%	1%	19%	2%
Received Oral from Men	6%	59%	6%	52%	8%	34%	3%	25%	2%	8%
Gave Oral to Women	69%	4%	57%	3%	44%	1%	34%	1%	24%	2%
Gave Oral to Men	5%	59%	7%	53%	8%	36%	3%	23%	3%	7%
Vaginal Intercourse	85%	74%	74%	70%	58%	51%	54%	42%	43%	22%
Received Penis in Anus	3%	22%	4%	12%	5%	6%	1%	4%	2%	1%
Inserted Penis into Anus	24%		21%		11%		6%		2%	

cal imperative—to have sex and give birth early and often is in conflict with the world we live in. The growing time lag between the observable physical changes that occur during puberty and the psychological and brain changes that occur during adolescence is very important and widely overlooked. As decades go by, our children begin to look like adults earlier, but are not prepared to function as adults until much later.

The disconnect between a mature body and mature thinking creates the illusion that our teens are adults when, in fact, they are far from it.

As we've discussed, the awakening of sexual interest, whether for members of the same or the opposite sex, generally occurs around the age of ten, though in reality the age varies widely. Because they begin puberty earlier and their brains mature faster (recall the white matter connections that are in place earlier in adolescence), girls usually begin to show interest in crushes and "not just friends" relationships before boys. This is evident in middle school, where girls spend more time than boys talking and texting about issues related to dating and relationships.

By around age thirteen, the majority of boys and girls have become actively interested in sex due to the hormones released into their systems. In addition to hormones, sexual urges in teens are also heightened by the "love/cuddle" hormone oxytocin, thought to be the key chemical trigger underlying emotional attachment between partners and maternal behavior in women. Oxytocin receptors are a dime a dozen in our reward circuitry, which means it has a strong influence over behavior, particularly teen behavior which is strongly reward-based.

Picture a pumped-up teenage brain, hungry to be gratified instantly, primed to respond to pleasure and reward, but lacking a fine-tuned frontal lobe to keep impulses in check and consider long-term goals and consequences. Suddenly, the brain is flooded with powerful hormones such as testosterone and oxytocin, and you've got a powder keg volcano on your hands, ready to blow. Adults may be baffled by the ferocity of "puppy love," but in the adolescent brain, these urges in the body can take the form of a full-grown and unleashed Great Dane.

When those reproductive hormones hook up with brain receptors that control and react to sexual stimuli, your teen may be overwhelmed and underprepared for the wild feelings that make him or her want to do the craziest things. Although it's popular in our culture to think about sexual motivation and behavior as simple and predictable (particularly in sitcoms, where men do ridiculous and stupid things to hook up with women), it's really not true, especially where the brain is concerned. Sexual feelings and functioning require coordinated activity in brain regions, from the motivational centers in the hypothalamus, to the memory-rich interactions between the hippocampus and the neocortex, to the integration of the many sensory regions used to generate sexual response. In adolescence, all of those circuits are being used in this way for the first time. The interplay can be quite shocking for teens, and it takes time to get all the kinks worked out.

Unlike when adults rationally (or at least more rationally than teens!) grapple with the swirling seductiveness of sexual arousal, teens don't have adult frontal lobes to help them weigh consequences and successfully negotiate the new terrain. The teenage brain is woefully undermanned when it comes to the powerful interplay of physical pleasure, interpersonal emotion, and relationship-building that sex brings. But teenagers' bodies keep insisting feverishly that they want sex. So they're confused, disoriented, and easily led astray. They're vulnerable to making bad decisions in the best of circumstances, such as when they're trying to decide whether to go "all the way" with a boyfriend or girlfriend. They're also perfect targets for clever predators and high-risk users who can seduce a kid into making terrible sexual choices which are not in their interest, and which can have lifelong repercussions.

By simply understanding and explaining the conflicting messages sent out by the teen brain, we can help our teens to step back for a moment and learn how to use their powers of rational thought. This moment may be all they need to make a decision that will save them, at the very least, some discomfort.

Abstinence or Contraception

"As much as I'd like my daughter to wait to have sex, I do want to be sure that she has safe sex if she and her boyfriend end up making that choice. How do I balance the 'wait until you're ready' conversation with the 'make sure you're protected' conversation?"

Can we stop our teens from having sex until their frontal lobes are fully developed and they can make good, informed decisions about whom to have sex with, what kind of sex to have, and what kind of sexual person they want to be? Given the powerful sex hormones working hard in the reward-driven teen brain and the relative lack of frontal lobe control, trying to prevent teens from engaging in sexual activity—or encouraging teens to talk themselves out of sexual activity by pledging abstinence—is often a losing battle.

Research does not suggest that unfettered and irresponsible sex is a good thing for teens, but it does show that it's a bad, possibly harmful idea to promote programs that fail to educate teens broadly and truthfully about sex and contraception. The US has the highest rate of unplanned teen pregnancies in the world; 5.6 percent of adolescent girls become pregnant, and 82 percent of those pregnancies are unplanned. This is more than twice the world average and ten times the rate of China and Japan. Why is the US number one in a category no one would want to lead the world in? It could be that contraception is less widely (or appropriately) understood and used in countries like the US, which is seeing a surge of "abstinence only" sex education rather than lessons on how to prevent unwanted pregnancy. The more socially accepted and available contraception is in a given society, the lower the rate of teen pregnancy.

Thirty-seven percent of adolescent girls in the US who receive sex education that focuses on contraception use effective methods the first time they have sex. Those who receive abstinence-only sex education use effective methods at less than half that rate. There seems to be an assumption that those who receive abstinence-only education or who take abstinence pledges will not have sex—or at least, will have less sex. This is not the case. In 2009, the journal of the American Academy of Pediatrics published a study of sexual behavior in teens, comparing those who had taken an abstinence pledge with those who hadn't. Five years after making the pledge, 82 percent denied having made it. Teens who took the pledge were just as likely to have premarital sex, to acquire sexually transmitted diseases, and/or to engage in anal or oral sexual behaviors than those who hadn't pledged. The number of sexual partners reported and the age when the subjects first had sex was

the same across both groups. There was one difference, however: fewer abstinence-pledgers had used birth control (including condoms) during the previous year or when they last had
sex. As a result, the authors of the study recommended that
those who have taken virginity pledges be treated as an at-risk
group for teen pregnancy when seen by their pediatricians, an
ironic outcome considering that the intention of abstinence
training is to lower the risk of teen pregnancy.

Teaching abstinence as the way to reduce teen pregnancy is
a little like teaching starvation as a way of avoiding weight gain.
It might work—at least, until you get hungry enough to gorge
yourself on whatever you find in the nearest refrigerator—but
it's not a healthy, practical, or wise long-term strategy. Our
brains are wired to pursue sexual gratification, and during
adolescence those urges are new and at the highest levels they
will ever be. Expecting a teenager to ignore them is like telling a person to stop breathing. Any approach to the promotion
of sexual health that fails to account for biological reality is
bound to fail. Add to the mix the struggling, underdeveloped
adolescent frontal lobes, and it's easy to see why so many uned-
ucated teens who take abstinence pledges forget about them in
the face of the tsunami of sexual thoughts that are washing up
on their shores every day.

Pornography

*"Is porn going to ruin my son's ideas about sex? Will he
ever be able to make intimate love with someone when his
introduction to sex is through such unrealistic portrayals?
Yikes!"*

Every time teens turn on their computers, pornography is at the tips of their fingers. As the brain is developing rapidly, so are teens' ideas of themselves as sexual beings. Can exposure to pornography during those years alter the trajectory of that development for the worse? Or for the better?

Back in the days of *Playboy* magazines under the mattresses, kids were told that viewing pornography (and, masturbating, for that matter) would cause blindness. Undaunted, a generation of teens indulged, and though many of them now wear glasses, few were struck blind. But recent studies support the concern that teens' views about sex can be altered by pornography. For example, a study of teens in Taiwan showed that exposure to Internet porn was associated with a greater acceptance of sexual permissiveness and a greater likelihood of engaging in sexual behavior.

A recent study of teens tracked their behavior for two years. Researchers found that males who were exposed to Internet pornography were more likely to develop permissive sexual norms, such as engaging in casual sex or premarital sex, two years later. The opposite was true for females, for whom early exposure to Internet porn actually predicted less permissive sexual norms after two years. Boys who were exposed to sexual media were also more likely to engage in sexual harassment two years later. Both boys and girls who viewed pornography were more likely to have oral sex or sexual intercourse two years later.

It appears clear that exposure to pornography leads to more permissive sexual attitudes among teens. But can pornography lead to an unsatisfactory sex life? It's one thing to have a relaxed attitude toward sex, but what sex means and how it translates into intimacy is also important. A purely recreational attitude toward sex may impair a teen's ability to build substantive relationships which are loving, healthy, and fun. Exposure to pornography does not seem to promote the development of an attitude that sex is only for recreation and not for relationship-building. And, in general, exposure to pornography does not have an effect on intimacy in relationships during young adulthood. Only teens who believe that the sex portrayed in pornography reflects real-world sexual relationships are more likely to have a recreational attitude toward sex. Thus, it may be better for parents to point out the contrast between real-life sexual experiences and sex portrayed in pornography than to try to eliminate all access to the online onslaught of porn.

Many parents also worry that if their teens watch porn, they'll become preoccupied with sex. The problem is, teens are supposed to be preoccupied with sex, so it's hard to tell the difference between what's healthy and what's not. Exposure to pornography does lead teens to think more about sex. Whether the act of viewing pornography itself reflects an unhealthy preoccupation is a more subtle question that has not yet been answered by research. Parents also worry that teens who seem very interested in sex will be more attracted to pornography, but that does not appear to be the case. In a study of teen sexuality and sexual thinking, those with greater sexual interest and thinking at the beginning of the study were no more or less likely to use pornography than others by the end of the two-year period.

Recent media coverage of porn and its effects has also raised concern about addiction to pornography. In our view, the term "addiction" is used far too loosely in the popular media, giving the impression that almost anything can be addictive. In fact, addiction is a very complex disorder that varies from patient to patient. It involves a combination of physiological, behavioral, psychological, and social components, and it is often accompanied by other psychiatric conditions. It's very important, particularly with teens, not to misinterpret pornography use or an apparent preoccupation with sex as addiction.

However, developments in the science of addiction and our new understanding of the adolescent brain do raise red flags about chronic use of pornography by teens. Viewing sexually arousing images activates the same reward-related brain circuits that are activated by addictive drugs, and sexual activity alters cells in the nucleus accumbens, a brain region involved in reward and reinforcement. We also know that the adolescent brain responds differently from the adult brain to certain addictive drugs (sometimes more powerfully, sometimes less), and that with alcohol the earlier a teen starts to use, the more likely he is to become addicted. It's reasonable to be concerned—not necessarily about pornography addiction in the medical sense, but about the possibility that the teen brain may be too powerfully affected by pornography. Given what we know about the highly reactive teen reward system in relation to alcohol and other drugs, it's important to consider the fact that frequent porn use may influence teens' attitudes and feelings about sex in unrealistic or unhealthy ways, but we must await the findings of future research.

Sexuality and Violence

Women between the ages of sixteen and twenty-four are the most likely to experience violence in relationships. As many as one in three adolescent females will experience abuse in at least one romantic or sexual relationship. Young men often attempt to exert control over their girlfriends, and many young women mistake their boyfriend's hostility, jealousy, and possessiveness as romantic and reflective of the depth of their love. This can be a destructive miscalculation, because early instances of domestic violence are predictive of problems like suicidal behavior and substance abuse, and may quickly lead to a self-perpetuating cycle which many young, smart, kind, and talented women (and men, for that matter) feel powerless to break.

During adolescence, power in sexual relationships is mixed up with underdeveloped capacities for impulse control, self-monitoring, delay of gratification, and planning. If teens don't learn acceptable ways to balance power and exert control in their intimate relationships, then unhealthy patterns in love and sex are likely to become part of their adult lives. Given the high plasticity of the adolescent brain, the memories and patterns that teens form during those years will influence their subsequent choices and ways of relating to sex and sexual partners into adulthood and beyond. That's not to say that one's sexual tastes and style get set in stone during the teen years (thank goodness!), just that early patterns tend to be well learned and remain influential well beyond adolescence.

Parents should closely monitor their teens for signs of possessiveness, frequent anger, or subjugation of feelings to keep a boyfriend or girlfriend happy—all potential indicators that a relationship may be heading into dangerous territory.

Talking to Teens About Sex

The study of brain development shines a new light on the challenges that teens face as they come to inhabit their sex roles and sexuality. An awareness of the powerful effects of newly elevated sex hormones on the brain combined with frontal lobe underdevelopment allows us to rethink our views on teen sexuality and to help teens develop realistic strategies for dealing with the upheaval they experience as their bodies are readied for reproduction.

For many parents, talking to their kids about sex is not high on the list of fun things to do. It's safe to say that few teens look forward to the day their parents sit them down to discuss sex, condoms, and sexually transmitted diseases. But these conversations are vital for both short- and long-term sexual health. Let's face it, you really don't want your teens to learn about sex exclusively from friends, pornography, the Internet, or other nondiscerning adults. Talking about these changes in terms of the brain (not just urges and emotions) may offer a sense of relief and eliminate some discomfort, moving the "birds and the bees" talk off the most dreaded list.

Chapter 8

DRUGS

Some drugs are used as medicines, and some are used for fun. Some are legal, some are illegal, and some are legal only after a certain age. Some are cheap, and some are expensive. Some are frowned upon, and some have achieved the status of a must-have daily (or hourly) ritual. But they are all chemicals that alter the chemistry of our brains—some for good, some for bad, some for both.

In this chapter, we'll discuss the drugs that are most relevant to teens, regardless of their social, legal, or medical status. The adolescent brain has several characteristics that enhance the allure of drugs and increase the chances that teens will try them. The teen brain is highly responsive to things that activate the reward system, and many drugs reward the brain very powerfully. Teens are also more likely to try drugs in the first place simply because their brains are wired to reach out into the world and try new things. Add the fact that their frontal lobes are less able to suppress impulsive behaviors, and they may not be able to control drug use once they start. For all of these reasons, our drug-saturated society represents a real risk for teens.

We live in the most medicated society in history. Drug pushers can be found everywhere, from nefarious street corners to TV commercials to our spam folders. How do we help our teenagers find out which drugs are appropriate, which drugs should be avoided, and what the consequence of drug use will be? First, it is necessary to suspend your bias one way or another in order to assess the risk of drugs to your teen. Of course, that may be easier said than done! Though you may have a difficult time preventing your teen from trying drugs, it is crucial to arm him or her with appropriate information about the risks involved. Given the high-stakes brain development that goes on during adolescence, it's surprising that we do such a poor job of educating teens about the effects of drugs on their near and long-term future.

The Power of Reward

You may recall that the reward system is made up of several small clusters of cells located deep in the brain. Whenever cells in this area are activated, dopamine is released onto cells in the brain's pleasure center, the nucleus accumbens. Once the pleasure center is pleasured, whether by an ice cream sundae, sex, or a line of cocaine, you're likely to repeat whatever behavior triggered the dopamine blast. Of course, cocaine will activate that circuit more powerfully than a sundae will, but the same biological mechanisms are in play.

One of the reasons that rewards have such a lasting influence on behavior is that reinforcement doesn't just feel good, it also helps to stamp in behaviors that the brain believes are

beneficial for our survival. When the reward system is activated, the memories created during that time will seem more
pleasant, whether they were directly related to the rewarding
experience or not. In most cases, this natural and adaptive
process reinforces the right behaviors, like exercising, eating
a good meal, snuggling with a loved one, or getting a paycheck.

This process can also work against us. When we're experiencing pleasure, we tend to like the people, places, and activities with which we are engaged, and we're motivated to return
to them even after the pleasing effect has worn off. Most recreational drugs have this type of associative power. While intox-
icated, people often develop feelings of affection for strangers.
If you're in a bar for any amount of time, you're sure to find
someone who has had one too many drinks confess eternal
and undying love to someone they've just met. Though these
feelings seem real at the time, they aren't as related to the
situation as they are to the rewarding properties of the drug
itself. By way of associative learning, drugs motivate us to do
more drugs, and to hang out with the people and in the places
where we do those drugs. In adolescents, for whom social relationships are paramount and reward is particularly powerful,
these effects can be consuming.

Studies of drunk and high rats corroborate a biological basis
for drug-seeking behavior. Given the choice between spending time in a room in which they usually get a rewarding drug
and another in which they don't, rats typically go to the drug
room. This explains why people have such fond memories
of their drinking experiences, even when they're full of bad
people who make bad things happen. Hanging out in a dude's
dank, dirty basement might not lead to the creation of fond

memories, but add alcohol and a bong and the basement suddenly becomes the reward room in the rat study. Memories of drinking or getting high in the basement will make our brains yearn for cold, dank, subterranean mustiness. And because teens are motivated by reward more than by punishment, they're less likely to imagine all the terrible things that might occur in that miserable basement, making them more likely to return than adults, thinking ahead to the consequences of their actions, would be.

The Addictable Teen Brain

Despite the high degree to which the teen reward system responds to rewards and the anticipation of them, those same brain circuits may also be less active in the absence of anticipated rewards during the teen years. This may in part be the cause of one of the hallmarks of adolescence, boredom. The feeling of restlessness that results from low reactivity provides healthy motivation for teens to leave the nest, but the combination of these two poles—a lowered level of baseline activity plus easier activation in anticipation of reward—also provides a strong motivation for teens to get out of the house and seek dangerous pathways to pleasure.

In addition to the dip in baseline reward system activity, heightened reward system activity in anticipation of pleasure, and a facility for learning, there are other changes taking place in the adolescent brain that put teens at risk for drug use and abuse. In Chapter 1, we discussed how, as teens mature, their behavior increasingly comes under the control of the frontal lobes. By keeping emotional drives in check and providing organizational skills, the frontal lobes come to guide behavior efficiently. For instance, a child might not see the reasoning behind a parent saying, "Don't eat candy now because you will spoil your dinner." Their emotions are likely to be so powerful that they end up throwing a fit. However, during adolescence, the idea of having dessert after dinner makes more sense, as the frontal lobes step up and are able to anticipate future goals, and to execute plans to achieve them. But until control has shifted completely, which occurs some-time in the late teens or early twenties, teens are going to have a tough time delaying gratification.

Using a drug once throws the brain for a loop, but it gener-ally recovers quickly. Like the rest of the body, the brain works best in homeostasis, an organ's normal, healthy level of func-tioning. Psychoactive drugs pull the brain off of its game for a while, but the body works hard to clean up and get things back to normal (these efforts are what cause hangovers). But after repeated drug use, the brain adapts in order to function as close to normal as possible even when it's being flooded with chemicals. This kind of adaptation, or learning, leads to drug dependence.

The ease with which the teen brain learns ensures that habitual drug use will become deeply engrained in brain cir-cuitry. Even if a teen cuts down on drug use when he reaches adulthood, it may be too late for the brain to get itself back on track. The end result may be a brain that responds differently to the drug for years, or perhaps decades, to come. This helps explain why the earlier a person starts to drink recreationally, the more likely he or she is to develop alcohol abuse problems that persist into adulthood. The brain has efficiently learned how to make alcohol a part of its everyday existence.

Tolerance is the brain's way of working around the repeated presence of a drug. The initial strong effect of a drug diminishes as use continues over time. As tolerance develops, the user is likely to take more and more of the drug, in order to achieve the same effect that it provided initially, thus increasing the chances of becoming addicted. Studies in animals have shown that adolescents become more tolerant more rapidly than adults.

Once a person stops using a drug, the effect resembles slamming a car into reverse while driving down the highway. Drug-associated feelings of pleasure and satisfaction are replaced by displeasure and dissatisfaction as the brain painfully struggles to reset itself to non-drug conditions. For example, a person who uses marijuana regularly in order to feel relaxed will likely feel agitated and anxious when she goes cold turkey. And a person who uses amphetamine or cocaine to feel alert and energetic will feel sleepy and depressed when he quits. Just as the brain learned over time to depend on the drug to function, it now has to learn how to function without the drug. Repeated use of any drug that alters thoughts and feelings in a positive direction sets up the drug user for some suffering down the road. This period of re-adaptation is called withdrawal.

Though we've just delivered a lot of disturbing information, there is a silver lining. The enhanced brain plasticity of adolescents lends itself to recovery. Research indicates that well-implemented substance abuse treatment works in adolescents, particularly when the patients are motivated to improve. The fact that the adolescent brain is built to learn can lead to a greater chance of addiction, but also to a great capacity to learn within the recovery process.

From Stimulants to Opiates: The 411 on Individual Drugs

Below are the top drugs used by teens, in order of their popularity. The bulk of current scientific research as it relates to the teen brain has been done on alcohol and marijuana. There is little or no research to date on how other drugs affect teens in particular, because it is both ethically and scientifically tricky to study the effects of powerful and potentially dangerous drugs on adolescents. However, we are able to extrapolate from the research that exists regarding adults and adolescent animals, and what we know about similar classes of drugs.

ALCOHOL

> *"My father and my sister are both alcoholics, so I am particularly sensitive to drinking. But I'm taken aback by how casual many parents are about letting their kids drink once they hit the teenage years. Am I crazy to be concerned?"*

Every time your impressionable teen turns on the TV, he's sure to see a beer commercial featuring scantily-clad women and guys having all kinds of fun. Now imagine that that commercial was for cocaine. How would you feel about this kind of advertising? Concerned? Angry? Horrified? From the brain's point of view, alcohol is a drug just like cocaine or marijuana or ecstasy. Only it's legal, and available at a store near you.

Teens are far more likely to use alcohol and to use it persistently than any other drug out there. By twelfth grade, more than half of teens have used alcohol, and more than 25 percent have used it in the previous month. If you or another first-order relative (parent or sibling) is an alcoholic, it doubles your teen's chances of becoming an alcoholic. Yet, because alcohol is legal for those over twenty-one and has become such an omnipresent social lubricant in our culture, many parents drink and don't think of it as a drug. For all of these reasons, critical information about alcohol and what it does to the adolescent brain is rarely discussed with teens, if it's discussed at all.

In the short term, regardless of the drinker's age, alcohol impairs learning, decision-making, impulse control, balance, language skills, vision, and, at high enough doses, the ability to breathe and to perceive when something is blocking the airway. Younger people are less susceptible to the sleepiness caused by drinking, and also less likely to lose their balance, but alcohol impairs certain cognitive functions, like learning and information processing, more powerfully in adolescents than in adults. This represents a double risk for teens, because they can drink more before feeling tired but also suffer greater impairment of information processing, decision-making, and judgment while drinking.

Even bigger problems may arise when alcohol's effects wear off. The activity of some neurotransmitters is so suppressed by alcohol that when alcohol leaves the system those transmitters become hyperactive. Those hyperactive neurotransmitters open channels in brain cell membranes, thus damaging or even killing the cells. It's possible that throwing these neurotransmitters into hyperactive hangover mode by repeated drinking accounts for the difficulties in learning, memory, and problem-solving that result from repeated bouts of drunkenness. The available research suggests that the adolescent brain may be more vulnerable than the adult brain to this type of long-term damage.

Doctors Susan Tapert and Sandra Brown at the University of California have examined the impact of alcohol abuse on neuropsychological functioning in adolescents and young adults. In one study, fifteen- to sixteen-year-olds in an inpatient substance abuse treatment program who had been sober for at least three weeks were compared to other teens who had used alcohol moderately but had no history of alcohol problems. Frequent drinkers (those who had one hundred or more drinking sessions as teens before entering treatment), particularly those who had experienced alcohol withdrawal symptoms, performed more poorly on tests that measured learning, memory, visual–spatial functioning, and other cognitive abilities.

In a long-term study of teens aged thirteen to nineteen recruited from treatment programs, Dr. Tapert and her colleagues found that teens who returned to drinking after the program experienced a further decline in cognitive abilities over the next four years and performed particularly poorly on tests of attention. Another study that followed subjects for eight years, from age sixteen to twenty-four, found that cumulative substance use, including alcohol use, impaired verbal learning and memory. Heavy drinking alone was associated with lower scores on tests of attention, and subjects who had experienced alcohol withdrawal symptoms showed additional deficits in abilities related to seeing and recognizing spatial relations.

The same authors have used fMRI scans to assess how the brain functions after repeated drinking during adolescence. When researchers measured brain oxygen levels of alcohol-dependent young women and healthy control subjects between the ages of eighteen and twenty-five while they tested memory and attention, the researchers observed a clear trend toward memory impairment. The alcohol-dependent women showed significantly less brain activity in the frontal lobes and elsewhere while performing the memory task. It seems that repeated drinking during adolescence causes the brain to be less capable of marshalling its usual resources when confronted with a challenging learning task.

In a particularly interesting study, young women with a history of heavy drinking experienced more cravings for alcohol when presented with alcohol-related cues, such as words associated with drinking, than did women without heavy drinking histories. So, heavy drinking during adolescence seems to make people more susceptible to alcohol advertising or cues associated with alcohol use later in life.

Because some research questions simply cannot be answered in human studies, we have to use animals to find answers. In rats, the hippocampus, which is prominently involved in the formation of autobiographical memories, is far more sensitive to alcohol during adolescence than during adulthood. Adolescent rats don't need to drink as much as adults before cell death in the hippocampus, frontal lobes, and other brain regions occurs. Alcohol also suppresses the birth of new neurons in the hippocampus more easily in the adolescent brain, stunting many aspects of brain function, including mood regulation, learning, and recovery from injury. Human studies support these findings; the hippocampus is smaller in alcohol-abusing teens than in healthy teens. It's unclear whether this is due to the suppression of cell birth, the death of existing cells, both, or an alternative factor. But the bottom line is clear: both human and animal studies strongly suggest that drinking is riskier in terms of brain function for adolescents than it is for adults.

The powerful negative effects of alcohol on the hippocampus in the adolescent brain explain why so many teens experience memory blackouts while drinking heavily. Roughly 50 percent of college students have experienced at least one blackout, and a survey of approximately 5,000 recent high school graduates on their way to college revealed that of the more than half who consumed alcohol in the two weeks prior to the survey, 12 percent had experienced at least one blackout.

Alcohol abuse during adolescence is also associated with a reduction in the size of the amygdala, which is involved in assessing threat and interpreting emotion, and in the corpus callosum, which carries messages from one side of the brain to the other. Alcohol also interferes with the maturation of connections in white matter (the insulated axons that carry messages from one cell to another) in the frontal lobes. Research with rats suggests that cells hampered by alcohol during adolescence only partially recover with prolonged abstinence. The negative effects of alcohol on white matter development explain why long-term alcohol abuse during adolescence produces such marked and lasting impairment in thinking and reasoning.

The earlier an adolescent is exposed to alcohol, the greater the odds that he or she will become dependent on it. This devastating fact, coupled with alcohol's long-term effects on teens, makes it our duty to accurately communicate the deadly nature of this drug, even while to many—maybe even to you— it may appear to be the most benign.

MARIJUANA

> "I smoked a lot of pot as a teenager and I still smoke some-
> what regularly. I would rather that my daughter not begin
> this unhealthy habit. But since I smoke, I need all the
> resources and information I can muster to convince her to
> do otherwise."

From *Easy Rider* to Cheech and Chong to Bob Marley to Snoop Dogg, it's been several generations since smoking weed, skunk, ganja, doobie, and boo became synonymous with rebellion, counterculture, and coolness—the very things that are ridiculously attractive to a huge chunk of teenagers. If you've managed to tune out today's teen culture, it may shock you to learn that recreational marijuana use remains very popular among US teens and young adults. By twelfth grade, 31 percent of teens have used marijuana and more than 15 percent have used it in the month prior to being surveyed. However, what kids are smoking today is definitely not your grandfather's marijuana. The levels of THC (the primary psychoactive ingredient in marijuana) have risen markedly over the years, from about 1 to 2 percent in the late 1970s to roughly 10 percent in 2009. Although more potent strains of marijuana have always been available, they are far more common now. This means that today's pot smokers are exposed to a far stronger version of the drug, and this adds to concerns about both the immediate effects of a single dose and the long-term effects of repeated use.

Our brains naturally make a chemical similar to THC called anandamide, after the Sanskrit word for bliss. Both anandamide and THC bind to cannabinoid receptors in the brain, which are widely distributed and fine-tune how neurons communicate with one another. What this means is that the brain has a natural, internal, and delicate system that can be powerfully stimulated by smoking or eating marijuana— though the concentrations of cannabinoids that reach the brain after smoking marijuana far exceed what our natural receptors are used to dealing with. This overstimulation of the natural system is what gives rise to the strong feelings and cognitive impairments associated with marijuana use. Nobody knows why we have cannabinoid receptors, though it can be entertaining to speculate—and because we have them, giving THC a specific receptor system to act on, the range of marijuana's effects is a bit more limited than those of alcohol. Still, it has strong negative effects on learning and memory, appetite, sleep, and the ability to divide one's attention in complex tasks like driving.

Studies show that THC disrupts learning performance in adolescent animals far more potently than it does in adults, and that this difference in sensitivity can be traced down to the level of individual neurons in the hippocampus. These are striking findings, because they indicate that, like alcohol, THC elicits fundamentally different reactions in adolescent and adult brains. This can be a good starting point for a rational discussion of pot with your teen; the potential that marijuana will hinder academic, social, and athletic success will likely resonate more than an emotional argument.

For years, there have been concerns that marijuana use by young people might increase the risk of psychological problems such as depression. However, it's been difficult to determine if marijuana use is the real culprit when problems emerge, because there are so many other elements in the lives of teens that can be psychologically challenging. Some studies indicate that the younger a kid starts using marijuana, the greater the risk of psychological problems. Naturally this should raise a red flag for parents of young teens who use marijuana.

Other research indicates that adolescents who carry a specific gene may be at risk for serious psychiatric symptoms, including delusions, hallucinations, and the emergence of schizophrenia later in life if they smoke marijuana regularly during their teens. This research is still emerging, and the actual number of teens who may be at risk for this effect may be small. But there's no way to know who carries the gene until it's too late, so any teen who smokes marijuana regularly should be aware that they are risking their future mental health.

While marijuana is not addictive in the classic sense (users do not develop the kind of craving that alcohol produces, and the signs of physical dependence are far less extreme), with heavy and repeated use signs of physical dependence can emerge. And some teens get into a pattern of use that can cause them to suffer academically, withdraw from social activities that don't revolve around pot, and get them in trouble with the law. So even parents who smoke (or are former potheads) should talk with their teens about the drug's potential dangers.

NICOTINE

> "When my son told me that his best friend started smoking, I nearly had a conniption fit. How can anyone smoke death sticks? Obviously teenagers don't think ahead to the future. I'm terrified my impressionable son will start smoking as well."

Everybody seems to understand the risks of smoking. Graphic commercials dominate the airwaves, anti-smoking campaigns have been common for the last forty years, and smoking is prohibited in most public buildings. Even tobacco companies are spending millions of dollars to help people quit and discourage young people from starting (not because they really care, but because they're forced to by law). Yet in 2011, 12 percent of high school seniors reported having smoked a cigarette within the previous month. Obviously youth smoking is a problem we have not licked, and that could be, in part, because the adolescent frontal lobes are not yet tuned to think carefully about long-term consequences. But there is some new research that might help teens grasp why smoking might be particularly dangerous for them.

The problem is not that nicotine has any particularly bad effects on cognitive functions, such as learning or problem-solving. But it is highly addictive, and if it's taken into the body in the form of smoke from cigarettes or as smokeless tobacco placed in the mouth, it can cause cancer.

Research has also shown that adolescent animals have greater sensitivity to the rewarding and stimulating effects of nicotine than adults, which is in line with what we've previously mentioned regarding the hyperactive teen reward system. When rats are trained to self-administer nicotine, adolescents will take much more than adults. Adolescent animals are also less susceptible to the uncomfortable effects that nicotine can have, like agitation. The result is that adolescent smokers often experience more of the rewards and less of the negative effects of smoking, which leads to more smoking and more tobacco addiction.

NARCOTIC PAIN MEDICATIONS

> "My daughter goes to a fancy boarding school. Recently she told me that lots of kids were taking OxyContin at parties. I know this is a terribly addictive drug and I don't want her near it. But it seems to be all the rage."

Look on the cover of any supermarket rag and you're sure to see some celebrity on the way to rehab for abusing narcotic pain meds. These drugs are all the rage with the rich and famous and have, not surprisingly, found their way into the hands of teens as well.

Next to marijuana, prescription narcotics like OxyContin,

Percocet, and Vicodin are the most common vehicles for teens to get high. Roughly 5 to 10 percent of tenth graders used prescription pain medications recreationally in 2011.

Narcotic pain medications are synthetic variants of morphine and codeine, which come from the poppy plant. Their primary clinical use is to blunt our perception of pain, but they also produce intense euphoria by activating opiate receptors in the brain. Narcotic pain medications are highly addictive. Because the opiate receptors in our brains change rapidly in the presence of the drug, it doesn't take long for dependence to emerge. Once that happens, the brain is hooked. Whenever the drug is not present, the opiate receptors register a state of deprivation and the user is highly motivated to get that next fix. This vicious cycle is very hard to escape. Opiates can kill a person with one dose. If our brain's opiate receptors receive too much stimulation from an outside source, they can actually shut down the parts of the brain that keep us breathing. Fortunately, there are drugs such as naloxone (Narcan) that can reverse this life-threatening effect, but it has to be administered quickly after an overdose. Over the last decade, the number of teenagers hospitalized for pain medication overdoses has more than doubled.

COLD MEDICINES

"I came down with a bad cold and went into our medicine cabinet, which typically has an array of half-used bottles, to find that all three bottles had nothing but a drop left in them. Through our teen parent bat sense, we figured out what had happened. And now we are extremely careful not

*only about what we keep in our liquor cabinet but about
what we keep in our medicine cabinet as well."*

Did you know that even as we speak, all over this country—
in fact, all over the world—teenagers are sucking down cold
medicines and cough syrup to get high? They're easy to use,
readily available, plus lots of them taste really good. In 2006,
a major government survey showed that 3.1 million Americans between the ages of twelve and twenty-five were getting toasted on stuff you're supposed to take when you have
a stuffy head, runny nose, or scratchy throat. Little do teens
know these drugs can be very dangerous.

The main psychoactive ingredient in cold medicines is dex-
tromethorphan, or DXM, which is readily available at the local
drugstore and in most home medicine cabinets, in products
such as Robitussin, Coricidin, and NyQuil. DXM can even be
purchased in a powder form on the Internet. Some websites
encourage the abuse of DXM and offer advice on the best way
to get high on it.

The effects of DXM vary depending on the dose, and range
from mild stimulation and perceptual distortions (changes in
how things look and sound) to hallucinatory out-of-body experiences. Users often divide the DXM buzz into four categories,
or plateaus, based on the dose. The first, and mildest, plateau
is reached by taking around 120 mg. Full-on psychosis, including hallucinations and delusions, is experienced at the fourth
plateau and requires roughly 890 mg. Coricidin, one of the
more commonly abused medications, contains 30 mg of DXM,
meaning that a typical user would have to take four or more
pills for a noticeable effect and about thirty to experience a

full-blown psychotic reaction. The strange, dissociative, and often pleasurable effects of the drug—the floating, peaceful, out-of-body experiences—probably stem from the effects of DXM on opiate and other specialized receptors in multiple brain regions.

As with any other drug, the DXM buzz has a price, and the price is a steep one. Beyond the immediate effects on thinking and alertness, side effects can be severe and include confusion, double or blurred vision, dizziness, slurred speech, loss of muscle coordination, abdominal pain, nausea and vomiting, drowsiness, rapid heartbeat, muscle weakness, and numbness in fingers and toes. Death is possible with very high doses.

Because DXM is found in more than one hundred different products containing a wide range of other chemicals, taking large amounts of cold medicine for the DXM means exposing the body to potentially toxic levels of other ingredients, such as acetaminophen (the active ingredient in Tylenol and Coricidin). Liver damage has been reported at doses of four grams of acetaminophen per day, so taking more than twelve pills of Coricidin for a DXM buzz is likely to damage the liver. Many common cold medicines also contain the antihistamine chlorpheniramine maleate and the expectorant guaifenesin, both of which have shown to be dangerous and even deadly at high doses.

While many young people abuse and even become hooked on DXM, it is estimated that more than one in three first-time users will find nothing enjoyable about the experience and will not come back for more. About one in ten people are considered poor metabolizers of DXM due to an enzyme deficiency, so tend not to like the drug. Unfortunately, they usually find this out the hard way—by using it and getting sick because their bodies are less capable of processing and eliminating it.

RITALIN AND ADDERALL

It's become more and more popular to treat conditions like attention deficit disorder and hyperactivity with Ritalin and Adderall, so an increasing number of teenagers have these drugs in their lives, and in their pockets. Being teenagers, they experiment with them and share them with their friends.

Ritalin (methylphenidate) and Adderall (a cocktail of amphetamine and dextroamphetamine) are stimulants, and were once used primarily for weight loss or a speed rush. While these drugs have a focusing effect on people with ADHD, they keep those without the disorder awake and alert for long periods of time. Stimulants can be safe and effective if prescribed properly and used in strict adherence to the prescription, but they are widely misused by teens looking to get high, control their body weight, or to pull an all-night study session. Thirty-one percent of college students reported having misused ADHD medications by taking larger or more frequent doses than prescribed or by using someone else's medication, and 26 percent had provided their medications to other students. A whopping 56 percent of students with a prescription for ADHD medication had been approached within the previous six months with a request to pass on their medication.

There is a thriving black market in these drugs, particularly among high school and college students in academically competitive environments. This trend has become prevalent enough that some have begun to refer to Adderall as Ivy League crack. The jury is out on whether the misuse of these drugs actually produces an academic advantage; although the procrastinator may be able to stay awake all night hopped up on stimulants and get that paper written, the likelihood that the paper will be as good as one planned out, written, and edited over several days is low. Of course, driven students have been getting high off caffeine for years, but the use of ADHD medications escalates risk to a new level. Teens using stimulants tend to sleep for shorter or longer periods of time than is natural or healthy for them, missing out on the normal sleep patterns and sleep stages. This change in sleep patterns affects their ability to learn and remember new material. Many adolescents who take stimulants off prescription also report feeling irritable and impulsive.

Stimulants can be addictive, in part because they cause dopamine to be released in the reward system. If taken as prescribed, the drug is released slowly and does not produce the kind of dopamine-induced euphoria that can lead to addictive behavior. But when use is unsupervised, these drugs may be taken in patterns that increase the likelihood of addiction.

SALVIA

> *"Until last week, I thought salvia was a lovely purple flower my neighbors had in their yard. But my son has just informed me it's the drug of choice for a new friend of his. Just when you think they're safe . . ."*

Until recently, in the United States anyway, nobody knew much about *Salvia divinorum*. But in recent years it's acquired quite a cult following among US teens. In 2009, nearly 6 percent of high school seniors had used salvia within the past year. In some parts of the country, it has joined the growing list of substances whose use or possession is illegal, although it remains legal in some states.

Salvia divinorum is a plant from the mint family that produces hallucinogenic effects. Its active ingredient is salvinorin A, which produces salvia's psychoactive effects and is one of the most potent naturally occurring hallucinogens. The leaves of the plant can be chewed or smoked. It is also possible to get a concentrated extract of the plant material that can be smoked or placed under the tongue (where there are plenty of blood vessels to absorb the drug). The main effects include depersonalization (feeling outside of oneself), laughter, feelings of levitation, colored visions, déjà vu, and anxiety. The effects come on within about a minute but only last fifteen minutes or less, though the user might feel subtle lingering effects for a few hours. Some users claim that salvia produces life-altering insights and visions.

The effects of salvia on the brain are poorly understood, but it's believed that the drug's hallucinogenic properties arise from the effects of salvinorin A on the kappa-opioid receptor. Like other opiate receptors, the kappa-opioid receptor participates in the pain control process; it also affects other aspects of cognitive function.

Despite the fact that salvia is still legal in some states, it can be a dangerous drug. Obviously, any drug that causes blatant visual distortions and a sense of being outside one's body can be frightening and dangerous, especially for those who are unprepared for such powerful (even if short-lived) hallucinogenic experiences. Many people who have used salvia report not liking the experience very much, so its potential for chronic abuse and dependence seems low. The long-term effects of salvia use are unknown.

MDMA (ECSTASY)

"I did ecstasy as a college student, and I can still remember how pleasant an experience it was. Because I'm an open parent, my daughter came to me and told me that her boyfriend suggested they take it together. On the one hand, I'm glad my daughter came to me. On the other, I'm convinced they're going to get some laced with something deadly. This is the definition of being between a rock and a hard place."

Ecstasy is one of the greatest names anyone ever invented for a drug. The problem is, it's only half accurate. Yes, if your teenager takes some high-quality MDMA, she will feel ecstatic. She will experience a warm, glowing, liquid feeling in her bones. She will feel compassion and empathy and love for everyone around her—even for herself. She will want to dance, talk, and make out with someone cute all night. But the other side of the coin to ecstasy is misery.

Ecstasy is a synthetic drug chemically similar to both methamphetamine and the hallucinogen mescaline. In 2011, 8 percent of twelfth graders and 6 percent of tenth graders had tried MDMA. Its danger arises from two factors: 1) MDMA creates very positive feelings of interpersonal openness and connection, which can be a strong motivator for repeated use; and 2) it kills brain cells.

MDMA causes the neurons that make serotonin to release their serotonin supplies and interferes with their ability to take the serotonin back to recycle and reuse, essentially causing a massive serotonin dump in the brain. This leads to increased feelings of well-being and empathy, combined with altered perceptions and mild hallucinations. The drug also triggers the release of dopamine, which leads to euphoria.

MDMA interferes with the body's ability to regulate temperature and can lead to death by hyperthermia. Once the drug wears off, the brain finds itself in serotonin debt. It can take days to regenerate the missing serotonin. For this reason, users often feel depressed for days after using ecstasy. The real danger is that when MDMA causes the neurons to dump all that serotonin, it damages their ends, or terminals. Once the terminal of a neuron is damaged, a process called "dying back" kicks in and eventually the whole cell dies. Although it's a simplification, some say that ecstasy produces "holes in the brain." In studies of nonhuman primates, four days of MDMA exposure caused damage to serotonin neurons that remained seven years later. Studies of human MDMA users have also indicated death of serotonin neurons.

Once serotonin neurons are gone, they're gone forever. The animal studies showed some evidence of limited replacement of serotonin connections, but the replacement circuits were incomplete. Since serotonin neurons are critical for

maintaining stable mood, their loss may have severe consequences. Most antidepressants work by causing these neurons
to release serotonin, but if the neurons aren't there the drugs
have nothing to work with, so ecstasy users risk ending up in
a state of depression on which drugs have no effect.

The one piece of good news about MDMA is that it is typically not addictive. It is such an intense high, and leaves people in such a state of depression and mood hangover, that most
people who use it only do so occasionally. However, since we
don't yet know what level of MDMA use would *not* cause damage, it is best to encourage your teen to avoid it altogether.

METHAMPHETAMINE

> *"With all the portrayals of meth on the screen, this is the
> one drug I'm most adamant about my son not trying. How-
> ever, we live in a small town and I know it's around. My
> son is very responsible, but he's also a try-anything-once
> kind of guy. What can I tell him to convince him that meth
> should not be tried, ever?"*

From the heartland of the flyover states to the backwoods of
the Appalachian mountains to the picket fences of the suburbs
to the neon lights of Broadway and Hollywood, making meth
has become a mom-and-pop growth industry in America. As
in all the strongest businesses, the consumer quickly becomes
a returning customer. Meth is one of the most seductive and
addictive drugs available in the world today. It makes the user
feel that his mind is razor-sharp, that he has enough energy
to climb a mountain, run a marathon, and write a dystopian

young-adult trilogy all in one day. Then comes the big crash: lethargy, depression, and black soul-sucking moods that can spur self-destruction and suicide. The meth-head just wants to do one thing: more meth. And so the sad cycle continues.

Methamphetamine is a potent and highly addictive stimulant, which causes an increase in the release of norepinephrine, dopamine, and serotonin. Its acute effects include increases in blood pressure and body temperature, increase in focus and alertness, improved mood, a big-time energy boost, and decreased appetite. At high doses, or with repeated frequent use, the drug can cause psychosis (hallucinations and delusions), intense anxiety, and paranoia. It is also a potent neurotoxin that damages dopamine-containing neurons in the same way that MDMA kills off serotonin neurons. While most people think of it as a dangerous street drug, it's also prescribed as a medication (under the name Desoxyn) to treat ADHD, or as a weight-loss aid. Its most common use, however, is recreational. About 2 percent of US teens report having used methamphetamine recreationally.

COCAINE

"My son has had a long history with marijuana use. He's also tried prescription drugs. We have been to see a number of counselors, and we've tried to deal with the problem head on. But we have been unable to curtail his drug use. Last week, we made him take a drug test and for the first time, we found traces of cocaine. Now I feel like we're entering a whole other ball game and I'm scared this is one we can't possibly win."

Cocaine has had a glorious, powerful, and deadly hold on American culture. Rock stars have sung about it, celebrities have snorted too much of it, and we have lost too many to overdoses of this crazy powerful drug. When your teenager snorts a line of coke, he will immediately feel like Leonardo DiCaprio standing on the prow of the *Titanic* with the wind in his face, exclaiming, "I'm the king of the world!" By the time he comes crashing down from the glorious high, he will feel more like the protagonist in Kafka's *The Metamorphosis*, just after he's turned into a cockroach.

Cocaine, a powder created from leaves of the coca plant, acts as a potent stimulant and appetite suppressant. In 2011, between 3 and 4 percent of US teens reported having used cocaine, with 2 percent having used it within the previous year. Cocaine blocks the reuptake of dopamine, as well as serotonin and norepinephrine, which leads to feelings of euphoria. It also stimulates the frontal lobes, causing increased focus and attention. A rock form of cocaine, known as crack, can be smoked, but most cocaine use by teens in the US is inhaled in powder form.

Both powdered and rock forms of cocaine are highly addictive, due to the intense euphoria and the short time it lasts, which trigger repeated use.

Keeping Your Teen Off Drugs

There are lots of ways to get the teen reward system going, some safe and some not. It's not helpful to suppress the normal adolescent urge to find new things to activate those reward circuits, but it is helpful to steer adolescents toward things that will give their reward system a blast without the risks of drugs. Remember that the teen brain is a learning machine that quickly masters tasks, from playing baseball to performing calculus equations to doing drugs. But it has no inherent way of knowing which of these activities is safe and which is risky, which will lead to a life of happiness and which will lead to rehab.

Of course, no parent can eliminate the chance that his or her teenager will want to experiment with drugs, precisely because teens are wired to seek out new (and especially rewarding) experiences. That's why it can also be helpful to encourage your teen to think of drug use as the equivalent of being at risk for a disease. If you're predisposed to heart disease, you should stay away from cholesterol. If you're predisposed to diabetes, you should stay away from sugar. Using these examples in an open, honest discussion about drugs tends to move the discussion away from emotions and rules and toward facts, consequences, and good, old-fashioned, smart, savvy frontal lobe decision-making. The information presented in this chapter will help your teen make wise choices and avoid being persuaded by drug myths they hear on the street or from some "cool" kid they want to impress.

As is the case with other threats to adolescent development, parents are the first line of defense in protecting teens from drugs. Given the sheer amount of confusing material available, it is not surprising that many parents approach conversations about drug use with serious trepidation. In this chapter we've covered the most important and relevant information about the effects of drugs on adolescents' developing brains. The truth is that teens are going to make their own decisions about drug use, and the more information they have at their disposal at times when those critical decisions are made, the better.

Chapter 9

VIOLENCE

Heads blown up and brains spewing, eyeballs gouged from sockets, limbs hacked off and blood spurting, atomic wedgies—these are just a few of the images teenagers are bombarded with in video games, on television, and in the movies. Add to this the "real world" issues of bullying and violence in the home or in the neighborhood, and you can see how violence has the potential to influence nearly every aspect of a teen's life.

We're just beginning to understand the role that violence—whether perpetrated on kids, committed by kids, or consumed on-screen—has on the teen brain. Exposure to violence, both in real life and on the screen, can have a powerful negative impact on adolescents by chronically activating the body's stress response, decreasing the reactivity of the brain to violence, and training the brain to solve problems with violence and hostility. Exposure to violence can cause kids to withdraw socially at a time when social interactions are important for shaping identity, developing friends and love interests, and learning to play well with others.

Should you actively limit your teen's exposure to violence

of any kind, including their beloved video games? Is this even possible? The answer is yes to both. We can and should be limiting violence in the lives of our teens. Arguments will ensue, you will be told what a horrible person you are and how you will never be forgiven, but your teen will be less aggressive as a result. If you can teach your teenager to navigate difficult social interactions without resorting to fists, knives, cudgels, or guns, he will be much better able to resolve conflicts without violence as an adult.

Bang! Pow! Pop!

Whether your teenager faces a bully on the playground, a mugger in an alley, or watches a typical night of television where heads are shot, chopped off, or blown apart, violence activates the fight-or-flight response, that series of biological alarm bells that motivates us to get out of a dangerous situation (see chapter 2 for an in-depth discussion of the fight-or-flight response). When the stress response is activated, adrenaline courses through the veins, the heart beats faster, blood pressure increases, breathing becomes more rapid, decisions are made more quickly, and the body burns fuel at a faster rate, giving us the energy we need to handle the stressful situation. In addition, cortisol, the body's main stress hormone, further boosts energy and cognitive function (including memory formation for the stressful event), and decreases sensitivity to pain. When your body is in the throes of the fight-or-flight response, you are at your most physically efficient, but the cost of that chemical rush is that shortly thereafter you feel tired, agitated, anxious, and perhaps even mildly disoriented. It is fine—and even helpful—to experience this rush once in a while, but repeated exposure can be toxic.

High levels of cortisol, such as those experienced when the stress response is activated by repeated exposure to violence, damages memory circuits in the hippocampus, the brain region that plays a critical role in turning new information into stored memories. Those same memory circuits are more sensitive to cortisol during adolescence than they are in adulthood, and there is emerging evidence that repeated exposures to cortisol during adolescence may cause the hippocampus to function improperly in adulthood. It has not been proven that repeated exposure to high cortisol levels damages the adolescent hippocampus permanently, but as we've discussed in previous chapters, it's important to avoid any kind of damage to the brain during this vulnerable period, when the brain is being molded and shaped by experience. Nor is it just memory function that is placed in jeopardy by the stress associated with violence. Heavy cortisol exposure also contributes to anxiety and depression, suppresses the body's ability to fight disease, and leaves your teenager vulnerable to a number of psychological disorders, including substance abuse.

For those who are exposed to violence only rarely, the stress response passes after the perceived danger ends and the only likely after-effects are uncomfortable memories. Unfortunately, chronic exposure to violence, and the physiological arousal that accompanies it, has negative consequences for the brain and may interfere with health and well-being.

Violence Short-Circuits Brains and Lives

If you are under the assumption that teenagers are less influenced by violence than younger children, you are mistaken. In children under the age of ten, exposure to violence has clear negative effects on physical and emotional health, including elevated rates of anxiety and depression, poorer school performance, a greater number of missed school days, and lower self-esteem, and it's now clear that teens experience similar problems. Researchers at Boston University found that children and teens who witness real-world violence often experience the following:

- Sleep difficulties
- Poorer performance in school
- Somatic symptoms (headaches, upset stomach, other physical complaints)
- Anxiety about separation from caregivers
- Increased anger and aggression
- Depression, social withdrawal, apathy
- Intrusive thoughts, memories, and worries
- Increased delinquent or antisocial behavior

Teenagers who witness or experience domestic violence in particular are more likely to become drug abusers, truants, gang members, and runaways, they are more likely to be sexually promiscuous or suicidal, and they are more likely to suffer from damaging emotions like shame, confusion, rage, and fear. Boys who grow up in abusive environments are more likely to use violence against their wives and children, and girls are more likely to enter into relationships where they are abused and victimized.

Violence also has visible effects on the brain. One of the principal goals of adolescent brain development is to sculpt circuits that allow for effective communication between emotion and cognition—between feeling and thinking. As adolescence unfolds, the frontal lobes improve their ability to communicate with emotional areas deep in the brain and, importantly, to control how emotions are expressed in behavior. Neurons in various brain regions reach out to one another and create circuits for processing information and regulating emotional expression. Glial cells insulate the neurons in these circuits, creating white matter tracts that ensure fast and efficient communication. Young adults in their early twenties who were exposed to verbal abuse in the home during adolescence show widespread abnormalities in the white matter tracts—specifically, the circuits that connect the emotional areas of the brain to the cognitive areas of the brain. Scientists believe that when the relationship between feeling and thinking is compromised, the disconnect can lead to long-term difficulties in controlling impulses and expressing emotions. This could be at the root of behavioral problems, including drug abuse, suffered by many young, verbally abused teens.

Physically abused children also show widespread abnormalities and deficits in brain structure and function. For example, a region of the frontal lobes critical in attention span and memory formation is significantly smaller in older children and young adolescents who have been physically abused. Indeed, adults who suffered physical, sexual, or verbal abuse during childhood have poorly functioning frontal lobes, which control things like memory, reasoning, attention, and impulse control. Often these deficits are not apparent on the surface but reveal themselves under times of heightened stress. In part, this is because the teen has developed behavioral patterns that protect him in the short term but compromise health, happiness, work, and the ability to maintain loving relationships

---

Sobering Statistics

A shocking number of kids in America are exposed to or are victims of violence. Murder is the second leading cause of death for US adolescents overall, after car crashes and suicide, and it's the leading cause of death for African Americans aged ten to twenty-four. According to data from the Centers for Disease Control and Prevention, an average of sixteen young people aged ten to twenty-four were murdered every day in 2007. That's one every 1.5 hours. Most of these murders involve guns. One study comparing the US with a number of other countries showed that young people in America are nine times more likely to die in a firearm accident, eleven times more likely to commit suicide using a gun, sixteen times more likely to be murdered with a gun, than kids in the twenty-five other countries combined. An estimated 3.3 million children and adolescents witness domestic violence in the home, and 30 to 60 percent of those children are abused themselves.

in the long term. This learning process, in which the child develops coping mechanisms for abuse, is called pathological adaptation.

Boys who have experienced abuse often become distrustful and aggressive physically and/or verbally. Girls are more likely to become withdrawn, isolated, and depressed or anxious, avoiding social engagements in an attempt to limit opportunities for further abuse. While this may work in the short term, in the long run withdrawal can lead to a condition called learned helplessness, in which the victim simply shuts down when things get too intense. This can be devastating for teens, who then have to face embarrassment or rejection without the resources to cope.

The Dangers of Desensitization

How many times can your teenager blow a character's head off, blood and brains spewing as he keels over dead, before violence and murder become just another recreation, like going bowling or shooting pool? How many prostitutes does your teenager have to slaughter before his brain is conditioned to think that killing women is just good clean fun? How many innocent victims does your teenager have to see hacked, sliced, or sawed to death before he starts to think of human beings as pieces of meat that can be used to satisfy his own desires? As on-screen violence has become more graphic and accessible to teenagers, parents have become increasingly outraged, demanding that restrictions be placed on violent material—with good reason.

Desensitization is a natural learning process that gradually decreases the strength of the stress response after repeated exposure to stressful situations. The brain is built to help us learn to survive, particularly during adolescence. If stress—of which violence is a particularly intense kind—is an ever-present part of the environment, survival will be hindered if the brain continues to respond with a full-fledged stress response. This tendency can be helpful, such as when learning to drive a car, asking a love interest on a date, or overcoming stage fright. Desensitization is also helpful for people who suffer fears and phobias that keep them from living life to its fullest. By slowly and incrementally exposing a person to the object of his fear, the brain's fear response calms down. As the brain learns that asking a pretty girl on a date does not warrant a flop sweat, uncontrollable shaking, or the inability to construct even the simplest sentence, the person becomes less uncomfortable, conquers the fear, and asks the girl out. This is good!

But the process of desensitization can also work against a person and become detrimental to the culture as a whole, particularly when it comes to violence. The more the brain is exposed to violence, the more it tones down its reaction. People who are desensitized to violence are less likely to perceive violence as appalling, and their emotional response to violence is less intense. Studies conducted in the 1970s show that the physiological arousal (such as increases in breathing and heart rate) evoked by violent TV images diminished with repeated viewing. Even brief, one-time exposure to media violence in a laboratory reduced the strength of a person's reactions to real-life violence. More recent studies have shown that while kids who are only rarely exposed to violence experience internal conflict when considering whether to use their fists (or in the worst cases, a weapon) to solve a problem, those who have been desensitized see violence as an easy solution. This reflects a dangerous shift in how the brain processes and responds to violence.

Scientists at Columbia University showed violent film clips to a group of twenty-five-year-old men. When the subjects first viewed the images, there was vigorous communication between frontal lobe areas (which control emotional reactions) and the amygdala (which reacts to fear and stress and sounds an alarm to signal danger). The more violence these men were shown, the less the circuits between the frontal lobe and the amygdala fired. This shows that exposure to media violence diminishes one brain circuit that's critical for correctly managing thinking and emotion in a crisis. We're still not sure at what point after the exposure to violence is eliminated the alarm system resets and returns to normal. But the fact that these twenty-five-year-olds, who had fully but newly developed frontal lobes, showed such reduction in the activity of those brain circuits suggests that a teen's brain—in which the frontal lobes and the circuits that connect them to the amygdala are still developing—may become even more compromised. Because they're built to learn quickly, they "learn" whatever life throws at them. Unfortunately, they don't select for good or bad information. If they're bombarded by violent imagery and lose their sensitivity to brutality, there's a chance they'll spend the rest of their lives battling the demons of violence.

Bullying

"My son is terrified of a kid in his class who seems to have a gift for spotting other kids' weaknesses. So far my son has pretty much stayed out of his line of sight. But he's so anxious about being targeted that he is losing sleep over it."

Not surprisingly, bullies are less sensitive to the suffering of others and will become further desensitized if they are not deterred. Small, weak, vulnerable, and defenseless kids are bullied every day all over America—punched, kicked, made fun of, called names with the language of hate, their heads shoved down toilets, or shunned and humiliated. There's a long and horrifying tradition of bullying all over the world, and it's only recently that the magnitude of this problem has become clear due to some high-profile cases.

To be precise, bullying is the act of imposing one's will on another person to repress or punish him or her. Physical aggression, threats, teasing, harassment, and manipulation of relationships are all forms of bullying. In many organizations such as sororities, fraternities, sports teams, and marching bands, violent bullying has become institutionalized in the form of hazing. Today, as many as 30 percent of kids are victims of bullying or are bullies themselves.

Girls and boys bully differently. Boys' acts of bullying are usually physical. Girls bully by spreading rumors, ruining reputations, and destroying relationships. Physical bullying peaks during middle school, but verbal bullying continues throughout the school years. There is now a new generation of teen cyber bullies who are using the Web to tease, torment, and torture from afar. (See chapter 6 for more information on cyber bullying.)

Bullying is bad for both bully and bullied. Both experience excessive physical and emotional stress, which leads to depression, sleep disturbances, and in extreme circumstances suicide. Bullies and those they bully also experience other problems, not only in the present but in the future as well.

WHO BULLIES AND HOW TO STOP THEM

"My daughter was shunned by a bunch of girls in her class. We told her to just ignore their bad behavior, but now I'm not sure if we made the right choice as more and more kids in her class seem to be jumping on the bandwagon."

The desire to be popular, have a successful love life, academic career, and cool friends becomes the focal point for many teenagers, and achieving these things requires a level of social competence and sophistication kids don't need during childhood. Some manage to climb the social ladder with brains, some with beauty, some with charm, some with athletic prowess. How we choose to climb through the ranks will depend on what we've learned and what we're born with. If they do it right, adolescents will get lots of opportunities to learn how to attract and keep loving mates, and to hone the social skills needed to survive and thrive away from the nuclear family.

Life experience has taught some kids that the best way to handle social interactions is to treat everyone as an equal.

Others have learned to be submissive and avoid conflict. Still others have learned that might makes right and that it's okay to verbally, physically, and psychologically hurt others in order to succeed. It's not only kids on the fringes—those who don't fit in or don't get the positive attention they need—who seek to dominate through bullying. Popular kids can be culprits, too. Researchers at the University of Connecticut have identified two categories of popular students. One includes students who are genuinely well-liked by their peers; the other is comprised of students who are popular but not necessarily well-liked. Popular kids liked by their peers tend to be kind, trustworthy, and sociable. Kids who are popular but not well-liked can embody positive social traits, too, but they tend to be dominant, arrogant, and aggressive in both physical (e.g., hitting) and relational (e.g., coercing) ways. Their social status is maintained by fear. Peers view crossing them as risky, so they are allowed a free pass to the top of the hierarchy, at least for a while. Adult bullies, from Tony Soprano to Napoleon, find their way to the top of the food chain this way as well.

No matter what kind of bully you're dealing with, the bullying itself is best dealt with quickly. If bullying helps a teen feel strong and empowered, those behavioral tendencies will be reinforced in the brain, and it's likely that he or she will continue to bully others. If a bully's tactics are ignored or endured quietly by the victim, the bully will be emboldened, because their bullying actions have been inadvertently rewarded. The highly reactive teen reward system pats the bully on the back with a brief release of dopamine and endorphins, triggering the frontal lobes to pay close attention and to memorize the behaviors associated with the reward. As we've discussed in relation to food and drugs, this process is designed to lead us to repeat behaviors that bring survival and success. Unfortunately, it works just as well in abetting bullies.

Television Violence

"I was watching the news the other night with my son. We were being shown images from a war-torn nation that were so brutal I had to look away. My son didn't seem in the least bit fazed and I had to wonder if he was so used to watching violence that he no longer found it disturbing."

Even kids who never get bullied receive a daily dose of violence. Whether during the evening news, cable series, or prime-time crime dramas, violence streams into millions of homes with a predictable daily rhythm. By the time American adolescents turn eighteen years old, it's estimated that they will have witnessed 200,000 acts of televised violence, including 40,000 murders. The rate of violence in televised programs airing between 10 and 11 pm increased 134 percent between 1998 and 2002, and the acts of violence depicted in programs shifted from less violent (fistfights or martial arts fights) to more violent (knives, guns, or other weapons). Data from more recent years is not yet available, but it certainly seems that our teens are being assaulted by more and more graphic images. The question is, does this make the teen brain more prone to violence and destructive behavior?

Scientists must study subjects over a long period of time in order to see whether their levels of violence and aggression are

associated with how much violence they've seen on TV. One
such study found that people who watched more TV violence
as children (six to ten years of age) were more likely to exhibit
aggressive behaviors fifteen years later. This was true for both
boys and girls, and the correlation was particularly strong in
kids who identified with aggressive TV characters and/or perceived the violence as highly realistic. In another study, 396
kids aged seven to nine were divided into two groups. One was
shown violent film clips and the other nonviolent film clips.
Both groups were then instructed to play floor hockey. Those
exposed to violent footage were more likely to hit, elbow, or
shove opponents.

In addition to simply promoting violence by pairing it with
entertainment and therefore reinforcing it, on-screen violence leads to desensitization. Over time, violent acts lose their
impact on the sympathetic nervous system and related brain
areas that generate surprise and fear if the acts are not followed by actual pain and suffering on the part of the viewer.
In one recent study conducted at the National Institutes of
Health, adolescents aged fourteen to seventeen were asked
to watch short clips portraying violence from various com-
mercially available DVDs. The researchers found that, over
just a single session in the lab lasting a few hours, the sympathetic nervous system and the brain areas that regulate it
became desensitized. In fact, researchers reported that having
college students watch nine two-minute video clips depicting
violence taken from recent movies was sufficient to supply
evidence of desensitization. As successive clips were shown,
subjects reported enjoying the clips more and sympathizing
with the victims in the scenes less. And that's after a total of

eighteen minutes of film! This evidence is bolstered by what we've learned about teens who play violent video games.

Video Game Violence

"My son and I seem to be in a months-long war over his video game use. To me, it is over the top. He spends a minimum of two hours a day playing games either by himself or with his friends. He tells me that most of his friends spend at least twice that amount of time and that I need to chill out. This is such a hard one for me since video games were not an issue when I was a kid. I just don't know what's normal."

In 1972, a video game system developed by German-born American engineer Ralph Baer was marketed by Magnavox as the Odyssey. Today, people wear watches that are more complicated than the Odyssey, but the concept was revolutionary at the time. Between the spring of 1972 and fall of 1975, Magnavox sold 350,000 Odyssey units. An additional 80,000 rifle packs were sold, which allowed users to play basic shooting games. Video games clearly scratched an itch in humans—particularly male humans, and even more particularly teenage boys. By the mid-1970s, the home video game revolution was in full swing, and it has swung spectacularly into cyberspace with a sophistication and levels of violence that are as astounding as they are disturbing.

Over the years, access to games and game systems, the array of games from which to choose, and the amount of time

people spend playing games have all expanded at an astonishing rate. In 2008, sales of game consoles and games amounted
to roughly $21 billion in the US and over $42 billion world-
wide. In 2009, Neilson Media Research estimated that 54 percent of US households (62 million homes) had a video game
console or handheld video game device. This is an increase
of 15 million homes from three years earlier. Now, with iPads
and iPhones, it's even easier to access and play these games
outside the home.

In case you haven't seen a video game lately, game play
has become jaw-droppingly realistic. As competition for the
sweet video game dollar has grown, games have increasingly
targeted the itch that people who buy them want to scratch.
In America that seems to include lots and lots of hardcore
violence. A recent study of the content of video games reveals
that half of all games, and 90 percent of games rated appropriate for kids aged ten and older, include acts of violence.

In some games with violent content, the violence is mini-
mal, like hitting pedestrians with a car (what's a few broken
bones?). In others, the violence is graphic and looks so physically real it can take your breath away. Whereas the Odyssey's
rifle pack allowed users to shoot simple objects on the screen,
many new games allow users to shoot, slice open, and blow
up realistic characters, often controlled by other users in the
room or over the Internet. The end result can be gory to the
max. With rapid advances in technology, the level of realism
in newer gaming systems means that the death, maiming, and
destruction in violent games is becoming increasingly intense
and lifelike. And the closer the games get to real life, the more
likely they are to affect kids' real-life experiences. That's why

the military uses video games to immerse recruits in simulated battlefield scenarios in preparation for real-life war.

Lots of average American teenagers spent the 2004 Christmas season running down pedestrians, carjacking innocent citizens, shooting people, and even picking up prostitutes. Sometimes they'd even kill the prostitute to get their money back. They were playing one of the most popular video games that holiday season, *Grand Theft Auto: San Andreas*. More recent games make *Grand Theft Auto* seem as harmless as an episode of *Sesame Street*. Consider the 2007 shocker *Manhunt 2*, from the maker of *Grand Theft Auto*. The player becomes Dr. Daniel Craig, an institutionalized scientist who must torture and kill his way out of the insane asylum to find out how he landed there in the first place. There are three levels of brutality you can inflict, depending upon how long you lurk behind your prey. You can administer a quick kill, or, if you linger a little longer, you can do fun stuff like rip out your foe's trachea. If you wait just a little longer, you can experience the joy of castrating your opponent. And in the last few years, many new ultraviolent games have involved the murder of children, either as an objective of the game or as motivation for acts of violence against other characters in the game.

There's an ongoing and spirited debate over whether such games affect players, and thus the culture as a whole, negatively. As it turns out, the issue of whether violent video games are toxic to development, and just how toxic, is much more complex than it might seem at first glance. If playing violent games made teenagers immediately go on violent rampages, the suburbs would be awash with blood and gore during the weeks after Christmas and the release dates of new games.

That is not the case. However, there is compelling evidence
that violent video games stoke feelings of aggression in children and adolescents and reinforce violent tendencies in those
who already have them. To make matters worse, even nonviolent games have been associated with increased aggression
in teens.

THE NEGATIVE REWARDS OF PLAYING VIDEO GAMES

*"When my son is playing a video game, the rest of the world
disappears. If the house were on fire, he wouldn't even know
it. And this problem seems like nothing compared to what
he's actually watching as he ignores everything around
him. It is sickening! How can this not be having a profound
effect on his mind?"*

Repeated exposure to violence in video games has many
dire consequences. It desensitizes players to violence. It
diminishes the significance and consequences of violent acts
by rewarding violent choices. In many games, succeeding
means becoming a proficient, ruthless, and conscience-free
killer. Because of the highly reactive adolescent reward system, the high points earned for kills are strongly reinforcing.
As players continue to be rewarded for virtual violent behavior in games that are increasingly realistic, it follows that their
attitude toward real violence will become not just less negative, but actually positive. And many of these games involve
coordinated killing orchestrated by dozens of players working
together, which reinforces violent action as a fun group activ-

ity at a time when the teen brain is learning how to pick and navigate social activities.

One recent study sought to answer whether playing games in which violence is followed by reward has a different impact than virtual violence which goes unrewarded. Male and female undergraduates played one of three versions of a car racing game for twenty minutes. In one version, players got points for destroying opponents' cars and running over pedestrians. In the second version, they lost points for doing so. In a third version, there was no violence at all, just racing. After playing, the subjects took the State Hostility Scale test, which asks subjects to agree or disagree with statements such as "I feel aggravated" or "I feel angry." Subjects who had played either violent game (rewarded and unrewarded), but not subjects who played the nonviolent game, showed an increase in hostile feelings. In a subsequent experiment subjects were asked to complete words based on the first few letters. Half of the word fragments, such as "KI_ _", could be completed to make aggressive words such as "KILL." Researchers found that subjects playing the rewarded version of the violent game were more likely than the other subjects to create words associated with violence and aggression. So at least immediately after playing a violent video game, feelings of hostility increase in young people.

Violent video games not only stress teens out by activating the fight-or-flight response, reward violent choices, and desensitize kids to violence, they also change players' attitudes toward other risky behaviors. In a fascinating study, researchers at the University of Pittsburgh selected one hundred males aged eighteen to twenty-one from the college population and randomly assigned them to one of two experimental groups. One played *Simpsons: Hit and Run* (low violence); the other played *Grand Theft Auto III* (high violence). Those who played the high violence game exhibited greater increases in blood pressure and more negative emotions, were less cooperative, and expressed more positive attitudes about drug use than those who played the low violence game. The blood pressure differences are particularly striking because a strong physiological response shows just how powerful the effect of violent game play can be on the brain circuits that control responses to fear and stress.

As the brain develops, a shift occurs in the way it reacts to video games. In one study, researchers examined brain functioning, including frontal lobe activity, in six children (aged seven to ten) and six adults (aged twenty-six to forty-four) while they played Donkey Kong on a Nintendo Game Boy, widely considered a nonviolent game. During play, the researchers observed increased brain activity in the prefrontal lobes of five of the six adults, but only two of the six children. Of course this could be due, in part, to the fact that the adults have more frontal lobe function in general, but it also suggests that as children develop into adults those rational frontal lobes make the video game playing a very different experience.

One way in which the experience might be different has to do with the balance of power between emotion and cognition, which shifts as the brain matures during adolescence. A teen who feels aggressive after playing a video game may be more likely to express that aggressiveness physically, by getting into a fight or loud argument, than an adult, who has the frontal lobe control to suppress the impulse. Similar research shows elevated activity in the amygdala, the brain region that processes emotional responses to threatening stimuli, in teens playing violent video games. As we progress toward adulthood, the frontal lobes become more and more involved in directing attention, strategizing, making decisions, making sense of our emotional reactions, and controlling emotional urges, so it makes sense that the frontal lobes would be less involved and the amygdala more involved in game play in children.

Other studies have shown a different twist to the balance between emotions and thinking. It seems that in experienced players, the thinking parts of the brain take over and emotional responses become dampened, or desensitized. One study focused on the cingulate cortex, which includes two smaller parts: the dACC, which is involved in thinking about emotions, and the rACC, which is involved in experiencing emotions. In a study of experienced video gamers, the dACC was activated during play while the rACC and amygdala— also involved in experiencing emotions, particularly negative ones—were suppressed, suggesting that playing violent games often leads people to *think* more about violent emotions but to *feel* those same emotions less strongly. This shift likely reflects and contributes to desensitization.

It is possible to alter the course of normal developmental processes, including the shift in how brains handle game play. This is what concerns us most about the potential effects of violent video games on teenagers: their gaming experiences may permanently alter how the brain responds to violence. It's healthy to be appalled by violence. If playing violent games makes kids less appalled by violence, this would be a bad thing for society as a whole.

Minimizing Violence

Researchers at Stanford recently conducted a study involving all the third and fourth graders at two elementary schools in San Jose, California. They wanted to find out how behavior changes when kids watch less TV and play fewer video games. Regular teachers trained by the researchers delivered eighteen classroom lectures about the nature of TV programs and the importance of spending less time (a target goal of seven total hours per week) watching TV and playing video games. Kids were asked to report their own TV and video game use for a week, and then participated in a TV turnoff, which challenged kids to keep their TVs and game consoles turned off for ten days.

Kids were then rated by their peers for their aggressiveness, their playground behaviors were monitored for aggressiveness, and researchers assessed how frightening the world seemed to the kids. Relative to control subjects, children in the TV turnoff group were rated as less aggressive by peers and were less aggressive on the playground—the result, apparently, of watching less TV and spending less time playing video games.

It's hard enough to control a child's TV watching and game playing, never mind once that child becomes a teen and starts watching TV and playing games on handheld devices and outside the home. These findings suggest that, at least for younger kids, less time in front of our TVs, computers, and game consoles is a good thing. The earlier we start, the easier it will be to curb the number of screen hours.

Parents should also discuss the content of TV and games with teens, and talk about the impact that violence can have on thinking, feelings, and even brain function. A talk or series of talks along these lines will probably go a lot farther with teens than restrictions that may be difficult or impossible to enforce. There are multiple rating systems for TV, movies, and video games that you can use to facilitate your discussion. Most parents are unaware of or don't pay attention to these rating systems. In a survey of 657 students aged eight to seventeen, seven out of ten reported playing games that were rated M for "mature." The majority of boys who played M-rated games said they owned their own. Only 25 percent of the boys surveyed said their parents had stopped them from buying a game due to its content and rating, and only 40 percent of the parents surveyed reported that they understand the video game rating symbols.

The video game rating system consists of the following ratings:

EC: Early childhood
E: Everyone
E10+: Everyone 10 and older
T: Teen
M: Mature (17 and over)
AO: Adults only (18 and over)

This system was created by the Entertainment Software Rating Board (ESRB), which was established by the Entertainment Software Association in 1994. While imperfect, the system is useful for telling parents (and teens) how inappropriate content might be. Unfortunately, the ESRB website warns that games played online might not have a rating, particularly when players themselves can create their own content. The fact that many games today are geared toward online play makes this an issue of ever-increasing importance, as we discussed in more detail in chapter 6, about socializing in the digital world.

AFTERWORD

Have you breathed a sigh of relief yet? Most parents do when they find out that not wanting to be seen with parents in public, constantly testing and sometimes breaking the rules, having trouble sleeping, being moody and grumpy and obsessed with drugs, high speeds, extreme sports, violent video games, and spending time with friends (and sometimes dangerous acquaintances), etc., etc., is . . . normal!

We hope that in addition to a sigh, you've also developed new expectations about your teen's behavior. The information we've presented doesn't excuse poor behavior, but rather provides a new way of understanding the differences between you and your teen. Understanding how different and undeveloped your teen's brain is also brings a deeper sense of responsibility for establishing and enforcing healthy and sustainable boundaries that route adolescents in the right direction and teach them how to make healthier choices. While parenting adolescents will never be easy, new science at least provides inspiration for surviving the unpredictable teen brain.

Helping Teens Take Healthy Risks

One of teens' most commonly lamented and dangerous tendencies is their desire to take risks. Because we know teens are built to take risks and that grounding them until they reach their twenties isn't an option, we've got to help them take risks that don't involve drugs, fast driving, unprotected sex, or the myriad of other activities that get teens in trouble every day. Fortunately, it's not that hard to help adolescents find low-risk ways to satisfy the urge to take chances. It may not be quite as simple as putting a basketball in their hands or signing them up for drama club, but when kids are busy doing things that scratch their itches, they tend not to look elsewhere for ways to draw blood by scratching too hard in the wrong places. For some kids, an occasional trip to an amusement park provides enough risk-taking to hold them over for a while. For others, if it isn't extreme, it isn't worth doing. Keeping these teens safe requires a little more creativity, and parents may have to come to terms with allowing their teens to explore more physically risky endeavors. Rock climbing (including the indoor version), mountain biking, whitewater rafting, snowboarding, and a host of other "helmeted" sports might fit the bill for more adventurous teens. Remember that the urge to explore and take chances during adolescence is often accompanied by a strong drive to be with friends and away from parents. A family bungee jumping trip, however extreme, just won't be the same as one with peers.

Teen centers can offer both adult oversight and plenty of opportunities for teens to stretch out socially and explore.

Many schools and school systems also provide opportunities for teens to be out from under direct parental supervision but still in a safe environment. For example, many offer "project graduation" nights, in an effort to give students a full night of fun in a safe environment, thus deterring them from partying on their own the night after graduation. In our community in North Carolina, parents and school administrators plan the project for months in advance, with activities ranging from hypnosis demonstrations to dodgeball tournaments, paired with free food and (non-alcoholic) drink. The festivities start about 10 pm and finish at 6 am with breakfast. It's a big project and takes plenty of planning, but the payoff is that the teens have a great time and parents know that they're safe and not out drinking and driving from party to party all night.

Because new research shows that popularity has an effect on risk-taking, it's important to encourage our teens to be satisfied with a few good friends, and to feel okay about being on the outside of the "cool" social circles. Sometimes teens are so caught up in being in with the in-crowd that they fail to see how many different kinds of social groups are available to them. Parents, teachers, and counselors could be helpful by pointing out the meaningful and fun friendships that develop in circles other than the one the teen is focused on, such as a recreational sports team, a service learning group, or a school club. Although teens might have a knee-jerk reaction against such suggestions, it's amazing how quickly they can attach to new activities and groups, and begin to feel better about their social lives once they give it a try. By doing so, you'll prevent your teen from feeling compelled to skateboard off a balcony into a dumpster, or make out with a future career criminal.

What More Can We Do?

Research shows that parents have more of an impact on teen behavior than they think. Teens pay attention to what their parents and other adults say—though they might not let on that they care—and often change their behavior and attitudes accordingly. So what can you do this minute/week/month/year to help your teen? Here are four things that everyone who cares about a teenager can do to make a positive change in his or her life:

- Call for an adjustment of middle school and high school start times. The changes in sleep that occur during adolescence make it harder for teens to get to sleep and get up in the morning. Research suggests that when school start times are shifted later by even an hour, good things happen in attendance, grades, and graduation rates.

- Help teens delay the onset of drinking. Just because parents drink a glass of wine at night for pleasure, or for their health, does not mean kids should drink at home—or anywhere else—as well. Research tells us that alcohol has a negative effect on the developing adolescent brain and that the earlier in life kids start drinking, the higher the likelihood of alcohol dependence.

- Monitor your teen's video game shelf and trash the videos that celebrate violence. Even though your kid might think you're cool because you let them play ultraviolent video games, it's unhealthy training for the brain and could desensitize your kid to violence in general.

- Demand that your teen's school ditch the sugary and high fat foods and beverages in its vending machines. The fact that the frontal lobes are still developing means that teens have a harder time than adults making healthy choices regarding food. These choices will inform what and how they eat for the rest of their lives.

Raising teens requires a team effort, so we hope that you'll pass this book on to your teen's teachers, coaches, pediatricians, and (drum roll . . .) even to your teen! Although this book is written from parent to parent, it will be equally valuable to teens. By reading about what's changing in their brains, teens will gain a better understanding of themselves, why they feel compelled to do what they do and why they sometimes feel so at odds with adults. We hope that teens will come away with an enhanced respect for their brains—understanding both their power and their vulnerability—and will be motivated to do what it takes to help them mature optimally. Once teens see that this book is an objective and even-handed representation of the science of adolescence, and not a tool with which parents will bang them over the head, it will help everyone adjust their expectations and get a little closer to walking in one another's shoes.

Acknowledgments

We would like to thank Arielle Eckstut and David Henry Sterry, the Book Doctors, for all their help. Their skills, savvy, energy, and unflagging good humor helped bring this book together in unexpected and exciting ways. Their writing made the book come to life and made it accessible to the general audience for whom it is most relevant. We would also like to thank our editors, Alane Salierno Mason and Denise Scarfi. They saw potential in our ideas, and advised us wisely and patiently throughout the writing process. Without their guidance, this book would not exist.

Further Resources

Chapter 1: Teens and Their Brains

Ackerman, Sandra J. "The Adolescent Brain—The Dana Guide." Dana Foundation, November 2007. Available at: http://www.dana.org/news/brainhealth/detail.aspx?id=10056.

Casey, B., R. M. Jones, and L. H. Somerville. "Braking and Accelerating of the Adolescent Brain." *Journal of Research on Adolescence* 21, no. 1 (2011): 21–33. Available at: http://www.ncbi.nlm.nih.gov/pubmed/21475613.

David Dobbs. "Teenage Brains." *National Geographic*, October 2011. Available at: http://ngm.nationalgeographic.com/2011/10/teenage-brains/dobbs-text/1.

Giedd, J. N., F. M. Lalonde, M. J. Celano, et al. "Anatomical Brain Magnetic Resonance Imaging of Typically Developing Children and Adolescents." *Journal of the American Academy of Child and Adolescent Psychiatry* 48, no. 5 (2009): 465–70. Available at: http://www.ncbi.nlm.nih.gov/pmc/articles/PMC2892679.

Schenck, J. *Teaching and the Adolescent Brain: An Educator's Guide.* New York: W. W. Norton, 2011.

Spear, L. *The Behavioral Neuroscience of Adolescence.* New York: W. W. Norton, 2009.

Wallis, Claudia. "What Makes Teens Tick." *Time*, September 26, 2008. Available at: http://www.time.com/time/magazine/article/0,9171,994126,00.html.

White, A. M. "Understanding Adolescent Brain Development and its Impli-
    cations for the Clinician." *Adolescent Medicine: State of the Art Reviews*
    20, no. 1 (2009): 73–90. Available at: http://www.ncbi.nlm.nih.gov/
    pubmed/19492692.

"Inside the Teenage Brain." *Frontline.* WGBH/PBS. Available at: http://www
    .pbs.org/wgbh/pages/frontline/shows/teenbrain.

"The Teen Brain: Behavior, Problem Solving and Decision Making."
    American Academy of Child and Adolescent Psychiatry. Available
    at: http://www.aacap.org/cs/root/facts_for_families/the_teen_brain_
    behavior_problem_solving_and_decision_making.

"The Teen Brain: Still Under Construction." National Institute of Mental
    Health. Available at: http://www.nimh.nih.gov/health/publications/
    the-teen-brain-still-under-construction/complete-index.shtml.

"Understanding the Mysterious Teenage Brain." *Talk of the Nation.* National
    Public Radio, September 20, 2011. Available at: http://www.npr.org
    /2011/09/20/140637115/understanding-the-mysterious-teenage-brain.

Chapter 2: Mental Health

Brinkman, W. B., S. N. Sherman, A. R. Zmitrovich, et al. "In Their Own
    Words: Adolescent Views on ADHD and Their Evolving Role Manag-
    ing Medication." *Academic Pediatrics* 12, no. 1 (2012): 53–61. Available at:
    http://www.ncbi.nlm.nih.gov/pubmed/22133501.

Forbes, E. E., N. D. Ryan, M. L. Phillips, et al. "Healthy Adolescents' Neu-
    ral Response to Reward: Associations with Puberty, Positive Affect and
    Depressive Symptoms." *Journal of the American Academy of Child and
    Adolescent Psychiatry* 45 (2010): 326–34. Available at: http://www.ncbi
    .nlm.nih.gov/pubmed/20215938.

Halperin, J. M., A. C. Bédard, and J. T. Curchack-Lichtin. "Preventive Inter-
    ventions for ADHD: A Neurodevelopmental Perspective." *Neurothera-
    peutics,* June 13, 2012 (e-publication). Available at: http://www.ncbi.nlm
    .nih.gov/pubmed/22692794.

Kalikow, K. T. *Kids on Meds: Up-to-Date Information about the Most Commonly
    Prescribed Psychiatric Medications.* New York: W. W. Norton, 2011.

Kraly, F. S. *The Unwell Brain: Understanding the Psychobiology of Mental Health*. New York: W. W. Norton, 2009.

Mana, S., M.-L. Paillere Martinot, and J.-L. Martinot. "Brain Imaging Findings in Children and Adolescents with Mental Disorders: A Cross-Sectional Review." *European Psychiatry* 25 (2010): 345–54. Available at: http://brainmap.org/pubs/ManaEP10.pdf.

Shatkin, J. P. *Treating Child and Adolescent Mental Illness: A Practical, All-in-One Guide*. New York: W. W. Norton, 2009.

"Attention Deficit Hyperactivity Disorder." National Institute of Mental Health. Available at: http://www.nimh.nih.gov/health/publications/attention-deficit-hyperactivity-disorder/complete-index.shtml.

"Child and Adolescent Mental Health." Website. National Institute of Mental Health. Available at: http://www.nimh.nih.gov/health/topics/child-and-adolescent-mental-health/index.shtml.

"The Developing Brain: What It Means For Treating Adolescents." National Institute of Mental Health, May 10, 2012. Available at: http://videocast.nih.gov/Summary.asp?File=17260.

"Teen Suicide." National Alliance on Mental Illness. Available at: http://www.nami.org/Content/ContentGroups/Helpline1/Teenage_Suicide.htm.

"Teenagers With Eating Disorders: Facts For Families." American Academy of Child and Adolescent Psychiatry. Available at: http://aacap.org/page.ww?name=Teenagers+with+Eating+Disorders&section=Facts+for+Families.

"Teens and Stress: Special Report." Video. *Science Nation*. National Science Foundation, June 20, 2011. Available at: http://www.nsf.gov/news/special_reports/science_nation/teensstress.jsp.

National Suicide Prevention Lifeline: 1-800-273-TALK.

Directory of local suicide hotlines, available at: http://suicidehotlines.com.

Chapter 3: Food

Frank, G. K., and W. H. Kaye. "Current Status of Functional Imaging in Eating Disorders." *International Journal of Eating Disorders*, April 25,

2012 (e-publication). Available at: http://www.ncbi.nlm.nih.gov/pub med/22532388.

House, S. H. "Nurturing the Brain Nutritionally and Emotionally from Before Conception to Late Adolescence." *Nutrition and Health* 19, no. 1–2 (2007): 143–61. Available at: http://www.ncbi.nlm.nih.gov/pubmed/18309773.

Maayan, L., C. Hoogendoorn, V. Sweat, and A. Convit. "Disinhibited Eating in Obese Adolescents Is Associated with Orbitofrontal Volume Reductions and Executive Dysfunction." *Obesity* 19, no. 7 (2011): 1382–87. Available at: http://www.ncbi.nlm.nih.gov/pubmed/21350433.

Park, Alice. "Teen Obesity: Lack of Exercise May Not Be To Blame." *Time*, November 9, 2009. Available at: http://www.time.com/time/health/article/0,8599,1936777,00.html.

Roizen, M. F., and M. C. Oz. *YOU: The Owner's Manual for Teens: A Guide to a Healthy Body and Happy Life.* New York: Free Press, 2011.

Shanley, E., and C. Thompson. *Fueling the Teen Machine: What It Takes to Make Good Choices for Yourself Every Day.* 2nd edition. Boulder, CO: Bull Publishing, 2010.

Sohn, Emily. "Body Image Concerns Hardwired Into Women's Brains." Article and video. *Discovery News*, April 16, 2010. Available at: http://news.discovery.com/human/women-body-image.html.

Stice, E., S. Yokum, K. S. Burger, L. H. Epstein, and D. M. Small. "Youth at Risk for Obesity Show Greater Activation of Striatal and Somatosensory Regions to Food." *Journal of Neuroscience* 31, no. 12 (2011): 4360–66. Available at: http://www.ncbi.nlm.nih.gov/pubmed/21430137.

"For Parents: Weight and Eating Behavior Problems in Teens." Article and audio. *Family Doctor.* Available at: http://familydoctor.org/familydoctor/en/teens/food-fitness/tips-for-parents-weight-and-eating-behavior-problems-in-teens.html.

"Take Charge of Your Health: A Guide For Teenagers." National Institute of Diabetes and Digestive and Kidney Diseases, Available at: http://win.niddk.nih.gov/publications/take_charge.htm.

"Teen Health: How Regular Exercise Benefits Teens." *WebMD.* Available at: http://teens.webmd.com/benefits-of-exercise.

Chapter 4: Sleep

Cline, John, PhD. "Helping Teens Sleep Better." *Psychology Today*, April 21, 2009. Available at: http://www.psychologytoday.com/blog/sleepless-in -america/200904/helping-teens-sleep-better.

Colrain, M. "Sleep and the Brain." *Neuropsychology Review* 21 (2011): 1–4. Available at: http://www.ncbi.nlm.nih.gov/pubmed/21259122.

Colrain, M., and F. C. Baker. "Sleep EEG, the Clearest Window Through Which to View Adolescent Brain Development." *Sleep* 34, no. 10 (2011): 1287–88. Available at: http://www.ncbi.nlm.nih.gov/pubmed/21966058.

Emsellem, H. A., and C. Whiteley. *Snooze . . . or Lose! 10 "No-War" Ways to Improve Your Teen's Sleep Habits*. Washington, DC: Joseph Henry Press, 2006.

Tarokh, L., E. Van Reen, M. LeBourgeois, R. Seifer, and M. A. Carskadon. "Sleep EEG Provides Evidence that Cortical Changes Persist into Late Adolescence." *Sleep* 34, no. 10 (2011): 1385–93. Available at: http://www .ncbi.nlm.nih.gov/pubmed/21966070.1.

"Delayed School Start Time Associated with Improvements in Adolescent Behaviors." *Science Daily*, July 8, 2010. Available at: http://www.science daily.com/releases/2010/07/100705190532.htm.

"Sleep and Sleep Disorders in Children and Adolescents: Information for Parents and Educators." National Association of School Psychologists. Available at: http://www.nasponline.org/resources/health_wellness/ sleepdisorders_ho.aspx.

"Sleep Helps Reinforce Memory." *Discovery News*, January 24, 2011. Available at: http://news.discovery.com/human/sleep-memory-brain-110124 .html.

"Teens and Sleep." National Sleep Foundation. Available at: http://www .sleepfoundation.org/article/sleep-topics/teens-and-sleep.

"WebMD FIT Teens – Relaxation, Stress Relief and Sleep Information." Available at: http://fit.webmd.com/teen/recharge/default.htm.

Chapter 5: Driving

Copeland, Larry. "Most Teens Still Driving While Distracted." *USA Today*, August 2, 2010. Available at: http://www.usatoday.com/news/nation/2010-08-02-teendrivers02_ST_N.htm.

Garner, A. A., P. R. Fine, C. A. Franklin, R. W. Sattin, and D. Stavrinos. "Distracted Driving among Adolescents: Challenges and Opportunities." *Injury Prevention* 17, no. 4 (2011): 285. Available at: http://www.ncbi.nlm.nih.gov/pubmed/21708811.

Mirman, J. H., D. Albert, L. S. Jacobsohn, and F. K. Winston. "Factors Associated with Adolescents' Propensity to Drive with Multiple Passengers and to Engage in Risky Driving Behaviors." *Journal of Adolescent Health* 50, no. 6 (2012): 634–40. Available at: http://www.ncbi.nlm.nih.gov/pubmed/22626492.

Simons-Morton, B. G., M. C. Ouimet, and R. F. Catalano. "Parenting and the Young Driver Problem." *American Journal of Prevention Medicine* 35, no. 3 Supplement (2008): S294–303. Available at: http://www.ncbi.nlm.nih.gov/pubmed/18702985.

Simons-Morton, B. G., M. C. Ouimet, Z. Zhang, et al. "The Effect of Passengers and Risk-Taking Friends on Risky Driving and Crashes/Near Crashes among Novice Teenagers." *Journal of Adolescent Health* 49, no. 6 (2011): 587–93. Available at: http://www.ncbi.nlm.nih.gov/pubmed/22098768.

Williams, A. F., and R. A. Shults. "Graduated Driver Licensing Research, 2007–Present: A Review and Commentary." *Journal of Safety Research* 41 no. 2 (2010): 77–84. Available at: http://www.ncbi.nlm.nih.gov/pubmed/20497792.

"Parents Are the Key to Safe Teen Drivers." Centers for Disease Control and Prevention. Available at: http://www.cdc.gov/parentsarethekey.

"Teen Driver Safety." National Safety Council. Available at: http://www.nsc.org/safety_road/teendriving/pages/teen_driving.aspx.

"Teen Drivers: Graduated Driver Licensing." National Highway Traffic Safety Administration. Available at: http://www.nhtsa.gov/Driving

+Safety/Driver+Education/Teen+Drivers/Teen+Drivers+-+Graduated
+Driver+Licensing.

"Teens, Cell Phones and Driving." *About.com Pediatrics*. Available at: http://
pediatrics.about.com/od/cellphonesandkids/a/05_cell_driving.htm.

Chapter 6: The Digital World

Aboujaoude, E. *Virtually You: The Dangerous Powers of the E-Personality*. New
York: W. W. Norton, 2011.

Burnett, S., C. Sebastian, K. Cohen Kadosh, and S. J. Blakemore. "The Social
Brain in Adolescence: Evidence from Functional Magnetic Resonance
Imaging and Behavioral Studies." *Neuroscience and Biobehavioral
Reviews* 35, no. 8 (2011): 1654–64. Available at: http://www.ncbi.nlm.nih
.gov/pubmed/21036192.

Carr, N. *The Shallows: What the Internet Is Doing to Our Brains*. New York:
W. W. Norton, 2011.

Dong, G., H. Zhou, and X. Zhao. "Male Internet Addicts Show Impaired
Executive Control Ability: Evidence from a Color–Word Stroop Task."
Neuroscience Letters 499, no. 2 (2011): 114–18. Available at: http://www
.ncbi.nlm.nih.gov/pubmed/21645588.

Giannetti, Charlene C., and Margaret Sagarese. "Safety for Adolescents
Online Social Networking." National Parent Teacher Association.
Available at: http://www.pta.org/topic_safety_for_adolescents_online_
social_networking.asp.

Han, D. H., N. Bolo, M. A. Daniels, et al. "Brain Activity and Desire for Internet Video Game Play." *Comprehensive Psychiatry* 52 (2011): 88–95. Available at: http://www.ncbi.nlm.nih.gov/pubmed/21220070.

Judge, A. M. "'Sexting' among U.S. Adolescents: Psychological and Legal
Perspectives." *Harvard Review of Psychiatry* 20, no. 2 (2012): 86–96.
Available at: http://www.ncbi.nlm.nih.gov/pubmed/22512742.

Klass, Perri, MD. "Seeing Social Media as Adolescent Portal More than Pit-
fall." *New York Times*, January 9, 2012. Available at: http://www.nytimes
.com/2012/01/10/health/views/seeing-social-media-as-adolescent-portal
-more-than-pitfall.html.

Pfeifer, J. H., and S. J. Blakemore. "Adolescent Social Cognitive and Affective Neuroscience: Past, Present, and Future." *Social Cognitive and Affective Neuroscience* 7, no. 1 (2012): 1–10. Available at: http://www.ncbi.nlm.nih.gov/pubmed/22228750.

Pujazon-Zazik, M., and M. J. Park. "To Tweet, or Not to Tweet: Gender Differences and Potential Positive and Negative Health Outcomes of Adolescents' Social Internet Use." *American Journal of Men's Health* 4, no. 1 (2010): 77–85. Available at: http://www.ncbi.nlm.nih.gov/pubmed/20164062.

"Cyberbullying." US Department of Health and Human Services. Available at: http://www.stopbullying.gov/cyberbullying/index.html.

"Online Safety Research." Microsoft Safety and Security Center. Available at: http://www.microsoft.com/security/resources/research.aspx.

"Teens, Cell Phones, Texting." Pew Research Center. Available at: http://pewresearch.org/pubs/1572/teens-cell-phones-text-messages.

"What Americans Do Online: Social Media and Games Dominate Activity." *Nielsen Wire*, August 2, 2010. Available at: http://blog.nielsen.com/nielsenwire/online_mobile/what-americans-do-online-social-media-and-games-dominate-activity.

Chapter 7: Sex and Sexuality

Chandra, A., W. D. Mosher, C. Copen, et al. *Sexual Behavior, Sexual Attraction and Sexual Identity in the United States: Data from the 2006–2008 National Survey of Family Growth.* Centers for Disease Control and Prevention, National Health Statistics Report no. 36 (2011). Available at: http://www.cdc.gov/nchs/data/nhsr/nhsr036.pdf.

Cheng, G., A. E. Buyken, L. Shi, et al. "Beyond Overweight: Nutrition as an Important Lifestyle Factor Influencing Timing of Puberty." *Nutrition Review* 70, no. 3 (2012): 133–52. Available at: http://www.ncbi.nlm.nih.gov/pubmed/22364156.

Gong, G., Y. He, and A. C. Evans. "Brain Connectivity: Gender Makes a Difference." *Neuroscientist* 17, no. 5 (2011): 575–91. Available at: http://www.ncbi.nlm.nih.gov/pubmed/21527724.

Guy, R.J., G. C. Patton, and J. M. Kaldor. "Internet Pornography and Adolescent Health." *Medical Journal of Australia* 196, no. 9 (2012): 546–47. Available at: http://www.ncbi.nlm.nih.gov/pubmed/22621132.

Lenroot, R. K., and J. N. Giedd. "Sex Differences in the Adolescent Brain." *Brain and Cognition* 72, no. 1 (2010): 46–55. Available at: http://www.ncbi.nlm.nih.gov/pubmed/19913969.

Luder, M. T., I. Pittet, A. Berchtold, et al. "Associations Between Online Pornography and Sexual Behavior among Adolescents: Myth or Reality?" *Archives of Sexual Behavior* 40, no. 5 (2011): 1027–35. Available at: http://www.ncbi.nlm.nih.gov/pubmed/21290259.

Margolies, Lynn, PhD. "Teens and Internet Pornography." *PsychCentral.* Available at: http://psychcentral.com/lib/2010/teens-and-internet-pornography/all/1.

Scheve, Tom. "10 Tips for Talking with Your Teen About Sex Without Embarrassing Them." *Discovery Health.* Available at: http://health.howstuffworks.com/pregnancy-and-parenting/teenage-health/10-tips-for-talking-to-teens-about-sex.htm.

Zuk, M. *Paleofantasy: What Evolution Really Tells Us About Sex, Diet and How We Live.* New York: W. W. Norton, 2013.

"Adolescent Sexual and Reproductive Health." World Health Organization. Available at: http://www.who.int/reproductivehealth/publications/adolescence/en/index.html.

"Facts on American Teens' Sources of Information About Sex." Guttmacher Institute. Available at: http://www.guttmacher.org/pubs/FB-Teen-Sex-Ed.html.

"How Male and Female Brains Differ." *WebMD.* Available at: http://www.webmd.com/balance/features/how-male-female-brains-differ.

"Puberty: Brain Changes, Strange Changes." Public Broadcasting System. Available at: http://pbskids.org/itsmylife/body/puberty/article6.html.

"Sexual Risk Behavior: HIV, STD, and Teen Pregnancy Prevention." Centers for Disease Control and Prevention. Available at: http://www.cdc.gov/HealthyYouth/sexualbehaviors.

Chapter 8: Drugs

Casey, B. J., and R. M. Jones. "Neurobiology of the Adolescent Brain and Behavior: Implications for Substance Use Disorders." *Journal of the American Academy of Child and Adolescent Psychiatry* 49, no. 12 (2012): 1189–201. Available at: http://www.ncbi.nlm.nih.gov/pubmed/21093769.

Doremus-Fitzwater, T. L., E. I. Varlinskaya, and L. P. Spear. "Motivational Systems in Adolescence: Possible Implications for Age Differences in Substance Abuse and Other Risk-Taking Behaviors." *Brain and Cognition* 72, no. 1 (2010): 114–23. Available at: http://www.ncbi.nlm.nih.gov/pubmed/19762139.

Jacobus, J., S. Bava, M. Cohen-Zion, et al. "Functional Consequences of Marijuana Use in Adolescents." *Pharmacology Biochemistry Behavior* 92, no. 4 (2009): 559–65. Available at: http://www.ncbi.nlm.nih.gov/pubmed/19348837.

Kuhn, C., S. Swartzwelder, and W. Wilson. *Buzzed: The Straight Facts About the Most Used and Abused Drugs from Alcohol to Ecstasy.* New York: W. W. Norton, 2008.

Rutherford, H. J., L. C. Mayes, and M. N. Potenza. "Neurobiology of Adolescent Substance Use Disorders: Implications for Prevention and Treatment." *Child and Adolescent Psychiatric Clinics of North America* 19, no. 3 (2010): 479–92. Available at: http://www.ncbi.nlm.nih.gov/pubmed/20682216.

Tapert, Susan F., Lisa Caldwell, and Christina Burke. "Alcohol and the Adolescent Brain—Human Studies." National Institute on Alcohol Abuse and Alcoholism. Available at: http://pubs.niaaa.nih.gov/publications/arh284/205-212.htm.

Wetherill, R., and S. F. Tapert. "Adolescent Brain Development, Substance Use, and Psychotherapeutic Change." *Psychology of Addictive Behaviors*, June 25, 2012 (e-publication). Available at: http://www.ncbi.nlm.nih.gov/pubmed/22732057.

White, A. M., and H. S. Swartzwelder. "Age-related effects of alcohol on memory and memory-related brain function in adolescents and adults."

Recent Developments in Alcoholism 17 (2005): 161–76. Available at: http://www.ncbi.nlm.nih.gov/pubmed/15789865.

"Brain and Addiction." National Institute on Drug Abuse for Teens. Available at: http://teens.drugabuse.gov/facts/facts_brain1.php.

"Drugs and the Adolescent Brain: A Conversation with Nora Volkow, MD." Video. Available at: http://www.youtube.com/watch?v=1jLUOoSHs6Q.

"Monitoring the Future." National Survey Results on Adolescent Drug Use. Available at: http://www.monitoringthefuture.org.

National Institute on Drug Abuse. Drug fact sheets. Available at: http://www.drugabuse.gov/category/product-format/fact-sheets.

Neurobiology of Adolescent Drinking in Adulthood Consortium (NADIA). http://nadiaconsortium.org.

Substance Abuse Treatment Facility Locator. Substance Abuse and Mental Health Service Administration. Available at: http://findtreatment.samhsa.gov/TreatmentLocator/faces/quickSearch.jsp.

"Teen Alcoholism and Drug Addiction: Your Teen May Be at Risk for Alcoholism and Drug Abuse, But How Do You Know What to Watch For?" *EveryDayHealth.* Available at: http://www.everydayhealth.com/addiction/addiction-in-adolescence.aspx.

Chapter 9: Violence

Anderson, C. A., A. Shibuya, N. Ihori, et al. "Violent Video Game Effects on Aggression, Empathy, and Prosocial Behavior in Eastern and Western Countries: A Meta-Analytic Review." *Psychological Bulletin* 136, no. 2 (2010): 151–73. Available at: http://www.ncbi.nlm.nih.gov/pubmed/20192553.

Douglas, K., and C. C. Bell. "Youth Homicide Prevention." *Psychiatric Clinics of North America* 34, no. 1 (2011): 205–16. Available at: http://www.ncbi.nlm.nih.gov/pubmed/21333848.

Ferguson, C. J., and J. Kilburn. "The Public Health Risks of Media Violence: A Meta-Analytic Review." *Journal of Pediatrics* 154, no. 5 (2009): 759–63. Available at: http://www.ncbi.nlm.nih.gov/pubmed/19230901.

Fisher, H. L., T. E. Moffitt, R. M. Houts, D. W. Belsky, L. Arseneault, and A. Caspi. "Bullying Victimisation and Risk of Self Harm in Early Adolescence: Longitudinal Cohort Study." *British Medical Journal*, April 26, 2012: 344. Available at: http://www.ncbi.nlm.nih.gov/pubmed/22539176.

Hammond, W. R., and I. Arias. "Broadening the Approach to Youth Violence Prevention Through Public Health." *Journal of Prevention and Intervention in the Community* 39, no. 2 (2011): 167–75. Available at: http://www.ncbi.nlm.nih.gov/pubmed/21480033.

Leung, Rebecca. "Can a Videogame Lead to a Murder?" *CBS News*, February 11, 2009. Available at: http://www.cbsnews.com/2100-18560_162-678261.html.

Manganello, J. A. "Teens, Dating Violence, and Media Use: A Review of the Literature and Conceptual Model for Future Research." *Trauma Violence and Abuse* 9, no. 1 (2008): 3–18. Available at: http://www.ncbi.nlm.nih.gov/pubmed/18182628.

Martsolf, D. S., C. B. Draucker, P. L. Stephenson, C. B. Cook, and T. A. Heckman. "Patterns of Dating Violence Across Adolescence." *Qualitative Health Research*, June 15, 2012 (e-publication). Available at: http://www.ncbi.nlm.nih.gov/pubmed/22707342.

"Bullying Prevention." National Crime Prevention Council. Available at: http://www.ncpc.org/newsroom/current-campaigns/bully-prevention.

Common Sense Media. Website which rates movies and games for age appropriateness. Available at: http://www.commonsensemedia.org.

"Timeline: Major US School and College Shootings." *NBC News*/Reuters, April 3, 2012. Available at: http://www.msnbc.msn.com/id/46933954/ns/us_news/t/timeline-major-us-school-college-shootings.

"Youth Violence Resources." Centers for Disease Control and Prevention. Available at: http://www.cdc.gov/ViolencePrevention/youthviolence/index.html.

Index

Page numbers in *italics* refer to charts.

About the Authors

Scott Swartzwelder (left) is a neuropsychologist who studies the ways in which alcohol and other drugs interact with the brain, and particularly with brain mechanisms of learning and memory during adolescence and early adulthood. He has published more than 130 scientific papers, written four books translating the science of drug actions into lay language, and has trained more than 50 scientists and clinicians. In addition he has created and taught several innovative college courses on brain mechanisms of memory and drug effects and has consulted extensively as a scientific advisor with a number of national institutes and departments as well as with numerous public education and policy organizations. In addition to his research, teaching, and clinical consultation, he now lectures and consults to promote effective education about the developing brain, alcohol, and other drugs and is a principal investigator with the Neurobiology of Adolescent Drinking in Adulthood Consortium (NADIA), which is conducting research on the long-term effects of adolescent drinking.

Aaron White (right) is a biological psychologist whose research has focused on the effects of alcohol and other drugs on adolescent brain function and brain development, adolescent substance abuse treatment, and the development of high school and college alcohol prevention and education initiatives. He joined the National Institute on Alcohol Abuse and Alcoholism (NIAAA) in 2008, where he oversees publicly funded studies on college and underage drinking prevention. To date, he has published nearly 50 scientific articles and book chapters and two books. He has appeared in dozens of educational videos, documentaries, radio programs, and television news programs, and has given more than 200 presentations on the topics of alcohol, other drugs, and adolescent brain development. Along with Dr. Swartzwelder, he helped create an online alcohol education course for college students, called AlcoholEdu, which has been completed by more than 2,000,000 students since its inception.